D0287860

WHEN
THE WAR
ENDS

WHEN THE WAR ENDS

STUART CHASE has been commissioned by the Trustees of The Twentieth Century Fund to make a series of exploratory reports on postwar problems. These are being published under the general title, "When the War Ends," and the books are to appear at intervals of a few months during 1942 and 1943. The first volume, *The Road We Are Traveling: 1914-1942,* explored basic issues and fundamental trends. This volume, the second in the series, lays down some economic specifications for the postwar United States. Later books in the series will examine more specific questions of postwar readjustment. The tentative list of titles follows:

1

The Road We Are Traveling: 1914-1942

2

Goals for America: A Budget of Our Needs and Resources

3

The Dollar Dilemma: Problems of Postwar Finance

4

Tomorrow's Trade: Problems of Our Foreign Commerce

5

Farmer, Worker, Businessman: Their Place in Postwar America

6

Winning the Peace

GOALS FOR AMERICA

A BUDGET OF
OUR NEEDS AND RESOURCES

Guide lines to America's future
as reported to
THE TWENTIETH CENTURY FUND
by
STUART CHASE

NEW YORK
THE TWENTIETH CENTURY FUND
1942

MANUFACTURED IN THE UNITED STATES OF AMERICA
BY THE ACADEMY PRESS, NEW YORK

FOREWORD

MONTHS BEFORE the United States went into the war, the Twentieth Century Fund decided to devote an increasingly large proportion of its resources to studying the problems of postwar readjustment. As a first step, the Fund retained Stuart Chase to write a series of books to give the public a stimulating and provocative picture of some of the problems which the United States will face "When the War Ends" (the title of the series). The entrance of the United States into the conflict has made these books even more timely. The first concern of everyone must be, of course, to win the war. But challenging objectives for the peace are dynamic aids to fighting morale.

The first volume of the series, *The Road We Are Traveling: 1914-1942,* was published in April 1942. It gave a moving and colorful picture of the revolutionary trends in our social and economic life which took place between the two world wars and laid down a sort of base line for a preview of the future. In this second book, *Goals for America: A Budget of Our Needs and Resources,* Mr. Chase puts into ringing words the demands which the American people are making for a better world after the war. Other volumes to come will deal specifically with the problems we shall have to face in meeting these demands—demands which imply a determination to maintain full employment and achieve the maximum use of our productive capacity.

This series is designed to provoke thought and to stimulate discussion. Mr. Chase has been given entire freedom of authorship. However, he has had the advantage of advice and criticism in preparing the manuscript from the Fund's Economist, Dr. J. Frederic Dewhurst, and several other authorities—for which both Mr. Chase and the Fund are grateful. But the opinions and conclusions expressed in these books are those of Mr. Chase. The Trustees and Fund staff have taken no position either for or against them.

In the field of postwar research the Fund has already issued a report entitled *Postwar Planning in the United States,* by George B. Galloway, which lists the agencies—both public and private—which are conducting research in the field of postwar reconstruction. A new and expanded edition will appear early in 1943. The Fund also is about to undertake a larger survey in the postwar field, which will deal with some of the central problems of the transition period and of the ensuing peace. This will be carried on in the usual Fund manner: by a research staff of economists who will prepare the factual findings, and a special committee which will, on the basis of these findings, make specific recommendations for action.

The Fund hopes that all these activities will contribute to a wide public understanding both of the unequaled opportunity of the postwar period and of the difficult problems it will present. The Fund is especially indebted to Mr. Chase for his challenging contribution to this end.

EVANS CLARK, *Executive Director*
The Twentieth Century Fund

CONTENTS

GOALS FOR AMERICA

A BUDGET OF OUR NEEDS AND RESOURCES

1

ESSAY ON SURVIVAL

SOMEDAY the bombers will be grounded, the bugles will sound, and the war will end. All-out, total wars cannot be maintained indefinitely. If the end comes within the next three or four years, the physical picture of the American economy promises to look something like this:

A vast force of trained workers in the war industries to be demobilized and shifted to peacetime occupations. They may be expected to insist vigorously on re-employment.

An industrial plant greatly expanded, especially for the production of machinery and such materials as light metals, rubber, other synthetics and plastics.

Machine tools—the machines which make machines—in great profusion.

An agricultural plant specializing in crops of high nutritional value, and capable of supplying far more than our own population.

A very great increase in electrical energy.

A vast budget of postponed wants to be filled—houses, clothing, automobiles, tires, radios, washing machines, durable consumers goods of all kinds. Incidentally, many consumers will have stored up purchasing power with which to buy them.

An insistent call from abroad for American food, supplies and industrial equipment.

An imperative demand for public works neglected during the war—conservation, hospitals, highways, schools, water systems, sewer systems, irrigation, transport facilities, and the like.

A promise of freedom from want to be redeemed.

Americans will find themselves with plenty of tasks to do. They will have the trained man power, the plant, the energy, the raw materials, the machine tools, to do it with. Failing a very long war which erodes away much of the plant, the outlook in physical terms is encouraging. There should be no material reason for not carrying American civilization forward, as well as supplying many victims of the war beyond our borders. We shall be physically equipped to do both.

Shall we be mentally prepared? Are we going to be flexible enough as a people to adjust our concepts so that these strong physical elements can be fully used? Will the war educate us to put first things first? Or shall we close our eyes to the physical realities as we did in the years after the panic of 1929? . . . That was a strange business. Let me try to refresh your memory of the picture in physical terms, as a horrible example of what not to do when and if a postwar depression threatens.[1]

1. Many economists believe that the stored-up purchasing power will produce a boom at the end of the war, with the depression to come later as it did last time.

The Lesson of the Depression

When the big gong sounded in the New York Stock Exchange on the day of the crash in 1929, not only did shares come tumbling down, but the American people proceeded to go mad. I mean mad—in the sense of making an irrational attack on their own survival. To those of us who did not suffer much in the depression, the language seems strong. Even those who suffered bitterly often found some way to explain their misery. But to an impartial observer from another planet, the word madness would have seemed appropriate.

Suppose we join this observer up in the stratosphere in a rocket ship freshly arrived from outer space. The ship is equipped with geophysical instruments of a precision and delicacy unknown on earth. With their aid, the observer can see land, forests, animals, farms, cities, factories, railroads, warehouses, stores, the inside of houses. He can see men and women moving, but he cannot see bank credit, mortgages, contracts, or the financial concepts which men carry around in their heads. Fine as are his instruments, they do not permit him to open a brain case and interpret the electric impulses which account for human thinking.

It is October 25, 1929. The observer sees a reasonably active continent. Nearly everybody has something to do. The comparatively few people he sees without work are either unemployable, or shifting from job to job. Farmers are in their fields harvesting crops for the market; industrial workers are at their machines and conveyor belts, merchants at their counters, railroad engineers at their throttles, bootleggers at their steering wheels. A vast torrent of goods is flowing along the highways, the railways and the waterways. Not many Americans are starving; not many are begging; none is on federal relief. Our observer has enough compassion to be shocked by some of the things he sees—the condition of many share croppers, the hopeless faces in textile towns whose mills have moved away, the black mining villages of Pennsylvania—but he notes that these are exceptions to an active population.

The observer takes his rocket ship home and returns two years later. He looks again, and finds it difficult to believe his eyes. What on earth are these people doing down there? Are they determined to destroy themselves?

Look! Millions of men have thrown down their tools and left their machines and conveyor belts in the factories; they drift around the streets doing nothing. The farmers' crops, harvested with such labor, lie rotting in the fields, or on railway sidings. There on a road a group of angry farmers has violently halted a line of trucks. They are pouring something white into the ditch—the milk with which the trucks are loaded. People are being evicted from their homes by the thousands in both city and country. They stand on the streets with little piles of household goods around them, and have no place to go. Most of the houses which they have left remain empty.

Men come stumbling out of mines, out of lumber camps, out of fisheries, railway shops, powerhouses, quarries, brickyards. Men and women leave their places in banks, offices, stores, restaurants, laundries, doctors' offices, moving-picture lots, to go home and sit staring at nothing. Structural steel workers climb down from half-completed skyscrapers, architects leave their drawing boards, engineers put away their blueprints, a great army of carpenters, masons, plumbers and painters hang up their overalls and fold their skillful hands.

People walk and walk, or they ride and ride in rattling jalopies on all the roads. They do not seem to get anywhere. A great army of boy- and girl-hoboes are riding the rods of freight trains. Some citizens are really starving now. A policeman picks up a man who has fainted in a doorway. He takes a girl from the railing of a bridge. Many children are staying home from school now, sitting at home without boots. In the reeking Chicago dumps back of the stockyards, men and women with little pointed sticks are raking the garbage for scraps of food.

Factories close one wing, then another, then bank their fires altogether. Mines flood with water, ships are tied up at docks, freight cars and trucks go into storage. There are few Pullman cars on the trains, and few passengers in those. Long lines of men move slowly up to gloomy buildings with signs saying "Soup Kitchen" or "Employment Agency."

By 1932, most of the vitality has gone out of this great country. In three short years production has been cut in half, and half the labor of the people is wasted in bitter idleness.

Is it any wonder that the observer thinks we have gone mad? He sees us crucifying ourselves *for no physical reason whatsoever.* No famines, crop failures, droughts or storms have overwhelmed us. No armed invaders are upon us. There stand the farms, the factories, transport lines, power centers, as strong as ever, ready to be used to produce as much as in 1929, and more. There stand the people, in dire want of the commodities and services they have stopped producing. It is like a farmer with fields full of ripe crops, who comes into the kitchen, slumps into a chair and tells the family there is no more to eat. Such a man would wind up in a state hospital. What are you going to do when it is not just one citizen, but a hundred million?

The Barrier of Tradition

We were not quite so mad as we looked. There was a reason. It was not a good physical reason, to be sure, but it was a powerful one psychologically. Our economic system for decades before 1929 had been operated on certain traditional customs, concepts and rules concerning markets, prices, debts, credit and money. The rules and concepts said that unless people had money they could not eat; if sales fell off severely workers would have to be discharged; if crops could not be sold farmers would have to destroy them; if rentals were not paid tenants would have to be evicted. We only followed our traditional behavior. We did not mount to the stratosphere to observe the insane effect on the American community viewed as a total organism.

Each citizen did what he could under these traditions. Very few citizens felt that they should be changed—at least not for the first year or two. Later on came many plans to make new patterns, some of them, like Technocracy and Social Credit, very unorthodox indeed. The old patterns were based on the theory of laissez faire, in which nobody is charged with seeing the economy as a whole. The economic system was supposed to be self-regulating, and it was considered "unsound" to monkey with the mechanism. When Mr. Hoover was first importuned to do something drastic about the crisis he said that "economic wounds must be healed by the action of the economic body—the producers and consumers themselves."

Nobody was responsible for checking unemployment and

deflation. Those evils were supposed to check themselves automatically—like an oil-burning furnace with a thermostat. Tradition said that when prices got low enough people would start to buy, prices would pick up, the "corner would be turned," and the unemployed would go back to work.

But this was a depression without a corner. Mr. Hoover and others were always thinking they saw a corner, but it wasn't there. The bottom of this deflation cycle was not recovery but complete disintegration. The collapse of the banks proved that. Some years later, the governor of a western state told me that he had considered seceding from the Union in late 1932. There were 400,000 citizens in his State in desperate circumstances. He proposed to seize the food and other physical supplies, with which the State was greatly blessed, and ration them to the population.

Under the rules and customs nobody could do anything about unemployment and starvation except in the most trivial way. Businessmen could do nothing about it, for as their sales and prices declined they had to dismiss their help or go bankrupt. Farmers could do nothing about it, for they had no money and no facilities to take their crops to market gratis. Investors could do nothing about it, for they could hardly launch new enterprises when the chimneys of most of their existing enterprises were cold. Labor unions could do nothing about it, for they had no plants of their own in which their members could work. Government leaders felt they could do nothing about it, for tax receipts were falling, making the budget harder to balance as it was, let alone spending for increased employment.

So it was all reasonable according to the ideas in people's heads, and quite senseless according to the laws of community survival in the physical world. Mr. Hoover was big enough finally to break some rules. He violated the sanctity of the balanced budget;[2] he put relief on a federal basis, and he organized the Reconstruction Finance Corporation to bolster failing banks, railroads and insurance companies. Mr. Roosevelt broke a lot more traditions. He abandoned the gold standard, pegged foreign exchanges, deliberately embarked on deficit spending for public works, took farmers out of the free market with the AAA, insured bank depositors against loss, and advanced government credit to citizens so that they would not be evicted from their homes.

Mr. Hoover recognized that somebody had to be responsible for the welfare of the American community as a whole. He was our first national planner in times of peace. The planning was neither extensive nor effective, but a new principle had been laid down. Mr. Roosevelt carried the principle much further. He did not cure unemployment, but his planning at least checked the downswing, and mitigated some of its most disastrous effects.

The war is breaking far more traditions and on a larger scale than ever the New Deal did. Price ceilings, priorities and rationing have obliterated what was left of the free market for the duration. Any private property anywhere can now be conscripted for the war effort. Listen to Donald Nelson speaking at the University of Missouri on June 9, 1942:

> America today is beginning to live under a war economy. Your most reliable routine will become suddenly valueless. No precedent

2. Government deficits were not invented by Mr. Hoover. Their history is a long and troubled one. But at best they have been regarded as a necessary evil.

is worth anything; the habits of thought which formerly meant success may now mean complete failure. The profit motive continues to exist, but it is no longer the mainspring.

There is not much left of the traditions we cherished so fiercely in 1929. By a curious irony, when we held to them in the early 1930's, production and unemployment continually became worse; when we broke some of them under the New Deal, production and employment rose; when we shattered them as we went to war, full employment was presently reached, while production climbed to heights previously undreamed of.

The Goal of Full Employment

Unemployment is the cancer of high-energy societies. In handicraft societies it is practically unknown. It is one of a very few hardships which people will not stand indefinitely. An economic system which leads to chronic unemployment, therefore, cannot last indefinitely. This senseless performance, of walking away from our places of work to rot in bread lines and on relief rolls, must not happen again. If we cannot make changes in our system in a democratic manner so that it does not happen again, a man on horseback will surely try to make them for us, perhaps with considerable mass approval. Hitler seized the government of Germany when unemployment reached one man out of three.

The most blatant and the most significant social phenomenon in the industrial system of our time has been unemployment. Everywhere it has persisted in the face of substantial economic recovery. . . . Whatever its causes—whether economic or political, too much or too little government interference, too much or too little rigidity, too much or too little speculation, too much or too little technical progress—unemployment is not an economic phenomenon, but first and foremost a social and political problem. . . . The unemployed person has no function in this economic life. . . . His existence is an irrational, incomprehensible one for society; and society itself loses all meaning to him. . . . We cannot expose our society to a repetition of such mass unemployment.[3]

The democracies have got to find a permanent way to full employment, and a way to give their citizens a sense of function, of *belonging* to the community. In this total war we are achieving both. After the war the process must go on. The most important goal for America, according to Mr. Drucker, is not a full quota of goods, not a fair division of property and income, not any material thing at all, but *work and responsibility,* so that citizens feel they are a living part of their community and not castaways beyond its gates.

The Goal of National Minimums

In 1929, America produced enough to keep most citizens supplied with at least the bare essentials of life. According to studies made by the National Survey, it could have produced some 40 per cent more than that.[4] Using the existing farm and factory plant, the Survey calculated the tonnage of physical goods which might have been made if management had been permitted to produce full out (as in the war, though working shorter hours) without regard to financial restrictions and market demand. The total would have given every

3. Peter F. Drucker in the *Virginia Quarterly Review,* Spring 1942.

4. *The Chart of Plenty,* by Harold Loeb, Viking Press, 1935. Based on findings of the National Survey of Potential Product Capacity (a government-sponsored organization). The Brookings Institution, using a different base, estimated in *America's Capacity to Produce* that some 19 per cent more goods could have been produced in 1929.

family in the country enough consumers' goods and services to provide a high standard of comfort and health.

All through the depression, output per man hour rose in most industries. The pressure to keep costs down resulted in many new laborsaving devices. Now the war is giving efficiency and scientific management another powerful stimulus. Mass production methods, we remember, were greatly accelerated during the last war. By 1945 or so our physical plant cannot fail to be far more productive than ever before, making the 1929 estimates grow faint by comparison. The outlook for the adequate provisioning of all Americans will be very promising when the war ends, as we shall see in some detail.

The physical factors will be available for a strong and enduring civilization. Will our minds be ready? No one can know. But my guess is that they will. This book is founded on the assumption that they will. On any other assumption it is not worth the writing, and we may as well compose ourselves to despair. Recently I had a letter from a camp follower of despair. He does not believe that rules should be changed, and so, of course, he sees the future as completely black. He wrote:

> It would seem impossible, after the war, to continue the same pace of production, for the limit of indebtedness and taxes may then have been reached. I do not see how unemployment can be avoided, and our people will have to accommodate themselves to a lower standard of living.

He is convinced that indebtedness and taxation will always control production and employment. Yet in a community devoted to its own survival, employment and production ought to control debts and taxation. First the physical realities, then the financial rules to help them work.

The Goal of Survival

> The minimum essentials for the maintenance of a community . . . are fundamentally biological; the first problems to be solved are those which will insure the biological continuity of the group. Biological continuity depends on the maintenance of a regular and dependable supply of organic necessities, and . . . demands the control of land, water and other resources found there. All social groups have provided themselves with an apparatus for getting physical necessities from their environment and for protecting the source of supply from the ravages of other groups, of other species, and of drastic natural changes.[5]

The authors of this passage are anthropologists who have observed primitive communities in action. They tell us, in effect, that any community without a firm will to survive is just another experiment which nature tosses into the waste bin of evolution.

The institutions and customs which the group develops—dealing with birth, marriage, the family, death, property, the technical arts, production, distribution, money, exchange—are always, to begin with, functions of survival. When environment changes, the institutions must change, or the community is headed for oblivion.

Consider a hypothetical community living in a protected valley, which regards it as wrong to kill human beings. This belief keeps down the homicide rate, and is good survival doctrine. Suddenly over the rim of the valley comes a horde of land-hungry warriors. Our community must now change its pacific institutions very rapidly if it is not to be wiped out.

5. W. L. Warner and P. S. Lunt, *The Social Life of a Modern Community*, Yale University Press, 1941.

The economic institutions America enjoyed up to 1929, while hard on some sections of the population, made on the whole for survival. Standards of living had increased for a century. Then the economic system began to go into reverse. It does no good from the biological viewpoint to argue about the moral virtues or the moral defects of the system which collapsed in 1929. It does no good to argue about the rights and wrongs of pacifism when invaders are coming through the mountain passes. The relevant fact is that from 1929 to 1940, the old system was inadequate to keep the American community afloat. Economic institutions must now shift, and allow enough economic planning to protect the community from such terrible ravages as that of the great depression. The depression of 1929 to 1940 was terrible in proportion to the stage of industrial development we had reached in 1929. The postwar depression, in a far more industrialized setting, will be correspondingly more terrible unless it is controlled.

President Roosevelt has announced that we must produce 125,000 war planes in 1943. They will be built by private industry, working to government contracts. Why can't we produce 1,500,000 houses in 1946, assuming that the war is over then, on the same general formula? Why can't the British rebuild their bombed cities after the war on the same formula? If we can achieve full employment by making tanks, why can't we achieve it by making schools? In physical terms, we can do it with ease. But some prewar institutions will have to move over, allowing a wider definition of the public interest. The change will be fully sanctioned by the principle of survival.

2
DUTIES AND RIGHTS

WHAT WILL BE the standards for community survival in the postwar world? The first consideration will be adequate military protection; but the extent of the military establishment will depend upon how the war comes out. If it ends in a balance-of-power settlement, the military establishment will continue large; if it ends in a smashing victory for the United Nations, it can be substantially reduced.

After defense, the next consideration for community survival is the complete, final and utter abolition of chronic unemployment. No nation which ignores this problem will have much of a chance in the postwar world. Whatever prewar rules interfere with its solution must be amended. Full employment obviously does not refer to the entire able-bodied population working eight hours a day for some employer on any given working day. It refers to a condition where every citizen who wants a job has the opportunity to connect with one, within a reasonable time, and with reasonable effort on his part.

The third task is the establishment of minimum standards of well-being for the entire population, so that citizens will feel reasonably secure, and, equally important, will be kept in physical and mental health. A nation of physical weaklings, of hopeless slum dwellers and tenant farmers, of white-collar workers in a perpetual agony of uncertainty about their jobs, their mortgages, their insurance and the future of their children—such a nation obviously cannot meet the stern requirements of the postwar world.

A fourth task is to hold natural resources at par so far as is physically possible. A nation which runs through its soils, forests, grasslands, watersheds, minerals, is certain to face a terrible day of reckoning. Here is one department where a modern nation can really go bankrupt.

Let us leave the subject of military planning to military experts for the present, and explore the second and especially the third steps in our program of national survival. How serious was chronic unemployment in the 1930's? What are the minimum standards of health and well-being for an American family? How many families have been below such standards in recent years, and in what specific items? How much would it take in goods and services to bring all families up to the minimum? Have we the plant and equipment to make good the shortages, and if so, how much margin above the basic line can be produced? What can our farms and factories be expected to produce when the war ends; will national minimums be harder or easier to meet than in the past?

The "People's Revolution"

These questions are not academic. We need the answers for practical reasons. Our armed forces need the answers, so that they can be sure they are fighting for a better world, not for a place in the bread line when the fighting is over. We need the answers to meet the urgent demands of a world revolution which nothing can stop. Henry Wallace, in a famous address, has called it the people's revolution.[1] "Everywhere," he says, "the common people are on the march. . . . The people's revolution aims at peace and not at violence, but if the rights of the common man are attacked, it unleashes the ferocity of a she-bear who has lost a cub. . . . If we really believe that we are fighting for a people's peace, all the rest becomes easy. Production, yes—it will be easy to get production without either strikes or sabotage; production with the wholehearted co-operation between willing arms and keen brains. . . . Modern science, when devoted to the general welfare, has in it potentialities of which we do not yet dream."

Sir Stafford Cripps, a few days earlier in London, sounded the same note:[2]

> The war has already resulted in many far-reaching changes in our national life. It will probably lead to more. Thus there is, in a sense, reconstruction actually in progress here and now, and this is all the more reason why we must not wait but continually work toward the end we have in view.
>
> There must not be after this war those gross inequalities that were the aftermath of the last war; none of the disgraceful contrast of great poverty and great wealth; no vast bands of heroic defenders of our country walking the streets in vain search for a livelihood. After the prodigious expense of life and wealth which this war will have entailed, the scourges of unemployment, malnutrition, unnecessary ill-health and waste of human ability, will no longer be tolerated.

Sir Stafford notes that the war is daily shaping the insti-

1. Before the Free World Association in New York, May 8, 1942.
2. Polish National Day address, May 3, 1942.

tutions of the postwar world. What is the shape of total war? It is a condition where every man, woman and child has specific duties to perform on behalf of his country. In return for these duties, every citizen is entitled to all the protection which the community can extend, share and share alike. Mr. Vanderbilt is allowed half a pound of sugar a week, precisely the same as a Mississippi share cropper. No citizen will long be permitted to go without adequate food, shelter, medical care. A similar shape must govern the postwar world if the people's revolution is to march on. It need not be so rigorous or so all-inclusive, but the basic pattern is clear enough.

The National Association of Manufacturers has not been noted for its endorsement of revolutionary economic changes. Yet a few days after Mr. Wallace and Sir Stafford had spoken, Walter D. Fuller, president of the Curtis Publishing Company and Chairman of the Board of the National Association of Manufacturers, warned four hundred Pennsylvania bankers at Atlantic City that the people's revolution was coming fast.[3]

> One thing is certain, the people of this country are fighting this war for a better world in which to live. They would like to get it through democracy, liberty and free enterprise. But they are determined to have this better world of greater security one way or another, and if they don't get it through present principles they will look elsewhere.
>
> The handwriting is on the wall. We either must cut the cloth to fit that pattern or the reformers and demagogues will. We can point to past accomplishments of free enterprise until hell freezes over, but people are concerned about the future, not the past.
>
> This country cannot return to "the good old days" after this war,

3. Reported in *The New York Times,* May 21, 1942.

> because those days just weren't good enough. They were the days when 28 million people were receiving some form of public assistance; when there were 10 million unemployed; when there was want amidst plenty. They were the days of idle money, idle men and idle plants. . . . Even in 1929 there were more than 42 families in 100 with incomes less than $25 a week.

This quotation deserves a second reading. Coming from this source it is a startling statement. Of course Mr. Fuller wants private enterprise to do the job. All right. The marching people and your author would be delighted to have private enterprise do the job, *so long as it is done.*

The *Fortune* poll for July 1942 gives a clear indication of what the mass of the American people want. They do not want a comprehensive system of "socialism"—25 per cent for it, 40 per cent against it, 34 per cent on the fence. But 74 per cent of them want medical care for everyone who needs it; 74 per cent want old-age pensions for every citizen over sixty-five; 68 per cent want jobs for everyone in public work if private work is not available; 58 per cent want unemployment compensation during the interim. They do not want incomes limited by law—60 per cent against, 32 per cent for—though they think that after the war there will be fewer rich people. Fifty-seven per cent want the government to regulate the banks, against 25 per cent who want the banks left alone. Majorities are against the regulation of automobile companies (59 per cent), and grocery stores (62 per cent).

Twice as many Americans believe that after the war life will be better than before, as believe the contrary; and more than twice as many believe that a young man will have more opportunity after the war than he had before. A substantial plurality believe that unemployment will be less five years after the war ends than it was in 1940.

If this poll is reliable, it is manifest that the majority of Americans are looking for a better world when the war ends. They do not want new "systems" or new ideologies, but they want jobs, public works, medical care and social security. They want the deed, not the word.

Freedom versus Order

Mr. Geoffrey Crowther, editor of the London *Economist,* gets down to fundamentals in postwar planning.[4] A strong believer in private enterprise, he doubts if businessmen alone can swing full employment and a guarantee of security for every citizen. He suggests the specific practices which must be changed. How, he asks, is it possible to set up an economic system which provides security without sacrificing political democracy? The central problem, as he sees it, is economic *freedom* versus economic *order.* With complete business freedom, guarantees of security are impossible. With complete order, business freedom flies out the window. "Our present mixture of freedom and order," he says, "does not work very successfully. But a balance of freedom and order could be contrived that would show a much better record." The province of an ordered economy should be universal minimum standards. Mr. Crowther would like to call these "The Citizens' Charter." (We will call them hereafter the Budget.) "It should include everything necessary to assure every citizen the essentials of a decent life." This is his list:

Food	Shelter	Clothing
Fuel	Education	Leisure time

Social Security, including unemployment,
health and old-age insurance

4. *Fortune,* October 1941.

"These," says Mr. Crowther, "are *rights* for every citizen." He notes how the "rights" went into action when Britain was first heavily bombed. Children were evacuated to safe retreats—the poor with the rich. Everybody was assured his fair share of food. Housing, medical care, air-raid shelters were made available to all. Clothing was rationed on a rigorously democratic basis. Air-raid wardens dug as faithfully for Mrs. Miller, somewhere under the ruins of her tenement, as they dug for the Duke of Wessex, somewhere under the ruins of his Mayfair palace.

This spirit must go on, says Mr. Crowther. "The community should openly admit what it has in fact practised for decades past; namely that there are certain forms of economic activity so important it is not prepared to allow the motive of profit to have the deciding voice in them." The Budget of necessities must be met, even if meeting it means in some particulars replacing the incentive of "freedom" with that of "order." Public schools, water supplies, highways, parks, public health services, have long been recognized as properly belonging in the domain of order.

Duties and Responsibilities

When he comes to duties, Mr. Crowther is equally emphatic. He believes that the Germans and Russians have been better organized than we have been in this department. They have elicited loyal effort from great numbers of their citizens. "They have grown powerful on the passionate devotion with which a whole people will embrace an opportunity to give service to their community." Whatever Mr. Crowther's evidence, or lack of evidence, for his strong phrase "passionate devotion," there can be little argument over our own need for such loyalty. The British people developed it magnificently during the blitz, and we have made our own beginnings under war pressures. But if the democracies are to disprove totalitarian claims, they must do so permanently. They must elicit even greater loyalty than have the Nazis and the Communists.

Mr. Crowther would have every young citizen give the community at least a year of his or her life. In the United States, Jerry Voorhis has introduced a bill into Congress along similar lines. A recent report of the American Youth Commission, headed by Owen D. Young, says that the government must see to it that all young people are constructively occupied up to the age of twenty-one. The obligation can be met by providing scholarships for talented youngsters, by expanding normal employment opportunities, by appropriate public works programs. We have had an outstanding example of the latter in the conservation work of the CCC camps. Over three million young Americans are graduates of these camps. Meanwhile every American male between eighteen and sixty-five has registered for national service. Women will probably follow. The idea of community service is readily accepted in wartime.

I quote Mr. Crowther at length not only because his views reflect my own,[5] but because they come from the editor of the London *Economist,* writing to the businessmen of America. Mr. Crowther believes that the democracies must prepare for national minimums *now,* and he is a very competent observer.

Defining the Budget

When the term "budget" is met throughout this book,

5. See Chapter VIII, A Budget, in the author's *Government in Business.*

the reader should be warned not to think of it as a financial statement, but as a balance between work, skill and plant on the one side, and the physical needs of the whole population on the other. It is the national budget of physical resources and requirements. Perhaps another term would have been better, but I am at a loss to find one. Mr. Crowther's "citizens' charter" does not seem to fill the bill, nor does Jeremy Bentham's classical "agenda" give us quite what we want. Remember when you see the word to think of men working and freight trains moving, not of dollar signs. The Budget as we shall use the term rests on four main points:

1. The *duty* of all citizens to render community service. This is primarily a matter of national psychology. Not everybody needs to be inspired at the start, but enough citizens must be inspired to make it morally odious for the unenthusiastic to withhold their contribution. The duty to serve would soon have the compulsion of public opinion. The duty might be discharged in one's younger years by serving in a national youth corps. Dorothy Thompson is working on a model with her Volunteer Land Corps. It might be discharged by making every citizen a kind of reserve national guardsman, subject to call in emergencies. The OCD is a preliminary working model. All active Civilian Defense workers are fingerprinted and carefully identified. Before the war ends this principle may be extended to the whole population, particularly if the rationing of supplies becomes general. We shall have to know who is entitled to what. Every citizen is counted and has his place in the community. Why should he not be identified and feel his responsibility in peace as well as war?

2. The necessity of maintaining *full employment.* This

point lies midway between the idea of duties and the idea of rights. Richard Roe has felt, does feel, and will feel, that he has a *right* to a job. It is one of the strongest feelings he knows. At the same time, unless Richard Roe is working at some task which contributes to community survival or comfort, the Budget cannot be achieved. So Richard has a *duty* to work. There is good reason to believe that the mass of Americans fear unemployment more than they fear any other social calamity; more than low wages, low living standards, poor food, ill-health.

According to the National Industrial Conference Board, average unemployment for both 1932 and 1933 was close to 13 million, with a peak of 14,762,000 in March 1933, the month of Mr. Roosevelt's inauguration. As late as March 1940, after the defense program was launched, the figure was 8,500,000.[6] This is a tremendous burden for any community to bear, but postwar unemployment could conceivably be worse. If we are devoting half our man power to military purposes when the war ends, and the government makes a sudden and drastic cut in military expenditures, half our labor force may be without work, unless civilian demand takes up the slack. Certainly it cannot be taken up overnight.

3. The right to a *national minimum* of certain essentials. For convenience let us call them the Big Five—adequate *food, shelter, clothing, health service,* and *education.* A definite tonnage of goods, and a definite allotment of services, under these five heads, would be available regularly to every family in the country. Most of the goods, of course, would be bought out of the citizen's wages. The point is that if he

6. Census estimate. The figure includes those on work relief as well as those seeking work.

cannot buy them, he should still get enough to keep him in health.

4. Examination of the *plant* which determines the variety and extent of the national minimums. What facilities does the nation possess to supply the needed goods in natural resources, skilled man power, technology, farms, factories, energy supply and transport? Will the Budget take all, or will there be a margin remaining for comforts and cultural goods after the necessities are provided for? Mr. Crowther estimates that in Britain, after the war, the margin will be as large as the Budget itself—50 per cent of all effort for necessities, 50 per cent for comforts and luxuries. The United States, remember, has a more productive plant per capita than Britain.

The estimates of requirements and supply which follow are based on physical things. You will not find many dollar signs in the whole discussion. We are going to strip the community to its fundamentals, and ask: What does it need in goods, what has it got to make them with? This is precisely the question which Mr. Donald Nelson is now asking, except that in his budget he substitutes guns for goods. He does not stop to worry about where the money is coming from, and neither shall we, in this study. We reserve that worry for a later book.

3
THE NATIONAL FAMILY

ONE WAY to visualize a National Minimum Budget is to think of all Americans as one big pioneer family. The family has passed over a range of mountains in the southwest, let us say, and come to rest in a fertile valley. Essential tools and seeds are in the covered wagons, and livestock has been driven over the mountain trail. Here are Pa, Ma, the sturdy sons, the younger children, assorted relatives, and some Mexican helpers. All the natural resources for survival are at hand—a stream of pure water, timbered slopes, rich bottom lands. Assume the family to be cut off for the time being from all contacts with the outside world. Life depends upon their own labor and skills. Within memory of living men there have been ranches and haciendas, in Texas and New Mexico, where conditions not far from this have actually obtained.

On Pa's ranch, it goes without saying, everybody works if he is going to eat. The children contribute to the family budget almost as soon as they can walk. The duties of every man, woman and child are clear. There is game to be hunted, fish to be caught, corn to be raised, houses to be built, firewood to be fetched, meals to be cooked, wool to be spun.

In our Great Family of 132 million members, we cannot say: "Work or starve," for civilized people do not let fellow citizens starve, but we might say: "Work or you will be taken to a sanitarium for the mentally unbalanced." Man, the biologists insist, is a working animal. For ten years, the overwhelming majority of our unemployed have been clamoring for work. Naturally we all prefer work which interests us, but even barren tasks are accepted in preference to the rot of idleness. When the time comes to adopt a definite procedure which gives John Everyman the choice, not of "work or fight," but of "take this job or lose your social security rights," a very delicate and difficult problem must be faced. Suppose John doesn't like the job, suppose it pays less than he thinks he is worth, suppose his union does not want him to take it? These questions cannot be dodged when the time comes. In a forthcoming study in this series, I shall try to face them. The responsibility of citizens to the community, and the responsibility of the community to them, is focused at this critical point.

Everybody works on Pa's ranch all right—though not, perhaps, with the hair-shirt fury of early New Englanders. The Mexican helpers make an admirable distinction between work which must be done and work as a variety of moral gymnastics. The latter philosophy escapes them. It also escapes me from time to time, despite my New England upbringing.

The American National Family

Who is in our Great Family? It includes some 30 million families, and perhaps 10 million single persons living alone. The following classifications were prepared by the Department of Commerce to represent the situation at the end of 1941:

Gainfully employed persons	50,000,000	
Unemployed (not on work relief)	4,000,000	
Housewives	29,000,000	
Total potential working force		83,000,000
Children under 14	31,000,000	
Students 14 to 25	9,000,000	
Old people, disabled people and people in institutions	10,000,000	
Total dependents		50,000,000
Total population (at Pearl-Harbor day)		133,000,000

The occupations of those working were as follows on Pearl-Harbor day:

In factories	13,000,000
On farms	10,000,000
In trade	7,000,000
In government	6,000,000
In finance and other services	4,000,000
In transport and public utilities	3,000,000
In the construction industry	2,000,000
In mining and quarrying	1,000,000
In all other occupations	4,000,000
Total as above	50,000,000

Thus some 83 million men and women, including housewives, support 50 million children, students in high school and college, old people unable to work, sick people and defectives, including criminals. The reason for classing housewives with workers and not with dependents is simple: because most of them work. Many work longer hours than their husbands. They are the mothers of the community, and from the standpoint of survival, they are the most important group there is. The idea that they are "dependents" is fantastic in any realistic appraisal, and shows how far money values have warped our judgment. Because a citizen does not punch a time clock does not mean that he or she is not a primary worker. If you told Ma on her ranch that she was a dependent, she would be justified in heaving a skillet at you.

Assuming an active force of 83 million working a 40-hour week, 50 weeks a year, that would give the Great Family 166 billion man hours of labor a year to provide the goods, guard the resources and run the national household. Before the war is over, we shall have an even larger draft of man power than this, as working hours rise. Perhaps as much as half the man power and more than half the materials will go into the war machine, yet none of us will starve on what remains. The total volume of consumers' goods will be about what it was in 1932, but the distribution will be far more equitable.

"A Single Unitary System"

To consider all Americans as one great household will not require a great effort of the imagination as the war increasingly invades our lives. Engineers and administrators in charge of the war program are more and more coming to think of the whole country as *one productive machine.* "To wage modern war," said Bernard Baruch in 1931, "is impossible without a sanction, control and leadership in industry sufficient to organize and deal with it as practically a single unitary system instead of a highly competitive community . . . only complete co-operation can procure supply in sufficient quantity." In the summer of 1942 we are already painfully aware of the truth of Mr. Baruch's statement. The American economy is gradually coming to be planned as a whole in terms of sequences. It is:

Useless to produce fighter planes if ships are not produced to move them to the battle fronts.

Useless to train pilots if planes are not produced for them to fly.

Useless to produce planes without producing pilots.

Useless to build aluminum plants if aluminum ore is not available.

Useless to produce tanks if the railroads cannot ship them to their destination.

Useless to build and equip machine-tool factories if skilled labor is not available.

First the goal must be clearly formulated—so many men, so much material, to arrive at specified places at specified times. Then the productive sequences must be worked out in advance, so that all parts move to final assembly in proper quantities—men, materials, energy and transport.

This procedure is unthinkable under business-as-usual, in which the community has no goals, except every man for himself. It is very difficult, accordingly, to get it going in democratic societies. They have had no experience with it. That is one reason why I have not yet ventured to criticize Donald Nelson. I know what a virgin wilderness he has to struggle through. Mr. Baruch learned the lesson in 1918, but it was soon forgotten.

This time it will not be forgotten soon because there will be no return to business-as-usual after the war ends, with 30 million men and women to be demobilized, and perhaps

Europe, Asia and Africa on our hands to feed or police or both. Can the goal of welfare replace the goal of winning the war? There is a fighting chance. The point I want to make, however, is that *we shall in fact be one great industrial family* when the war ends. We shall be operating as a single unified organism, and many of us will be thinking in those terms.

When the war began, the Army and Navy proceeded to secure triple A priorities on nearly everything in sight. Pretty soon the civilian population would have been faced—in 1943 or so—with prison fare if not outright pernicious anemia. This made no sense, for a total army in a total war is no good without a total people behind it. So in the summer of 1942, a new policy was put into effect whereby the health and morale of the people were given a priority rating too. In some cases military demands were cut in favor of civil. The civilian budget is to be stripped progressively to stark essentials, but the essentials are planned to reach every family in the nation.

From the standpoint of a balanced diet the U.S. will be as well fed in 1943 as ever before—if not better. We shall be long on wheat, eggs, dairy products, fruits and vegetables, short on sugar, coffee, tea, cocoa, tapioca, bananas and other imported foods. Clothing will be simpler, more standardized, as befits a war era, but to the extent that the U.S. has ever been well clad, it will continue to be well clad. Housing will be worse in the congested areas of war industry, but priorities have been issued for 670,000 new dwelling units, and "the government hopes to provide another 650,000 units by converting business properties, and remodeling old housing." There will be no new refrigerators, radios, toasters, vacuum cleaners. There will be less choice in kitchen pots, carpets, furniture. There may be some curtailment in electric power for home use, and in telephone calls. The production of fancy luxuries will cease, but there will be plenty of movies, cigarettes and reading matter. Travel for pleasure has already taken a sock in the eye.

Thus, due to elaborate government direction, people at the bottom of the economic ladder will live better in 1943 than they did in 1932. People at the top of the ladder will have to forego many of the luxuries they enjoyed in 1932. A vast leveling process is at work. It paves the way, and establishes the administrative techniques, for the era of national minimums which may come after the war.

The Big Five

The five great categories of minimum standards are food, shelter, clothing, health services and education. Let us examine each one of this "big five" and determine, so far as estimates are available, the Great Family's basic *needs,* the amounts being *supplied* (before war controls set in), and the extent of the gap between needs and supply. What will it take to close the gap? These studies will be carried out, as I said earlier, in the physical frame of reference.

The Twentieth Century Fund is engaged on a comprehensive study of the Budget with much detailed research. When completed the study will tell us what our productive capacity was before the war, and estimate what it promises to be after the war, to what extent basic wants can be met, and what will be left over for comforts and luxuries. I am conducting a preliminary survey in this little book, using the best figures and estimates I can find. Both studies are faced with the necessity of defining human wants, a subject philosophers have argued about for centuries.

> A book of verses underneath the bough,
> A jug of wine, a loaf of bread, and thou
> Beside me, singing in the wilderness;
> Ah, wilderness were paradise enow.

Well, maybe. Our postwar paradise promises to be a little more complicated. The loaf of bread is all right, but the jug of wine is optional. I am going chiefly to discuss basic wants, the loaf of bread idea. "The total consumption of necessaries," says E. H. Carr,[1] "varies with the number of the population; of luxuries with the extent of their purchasing power. Once an article is firmly established in the category of necessaries, further rises in the standard of living do little to increase the volume of consumption."

We shall confine ourselves in the following pages to those articles which vary with the population, and which do not tend to expand much when the individual *who already has them* finds his income expanding. The outstanding example is food. One can eat only so much. One can eat with more frills, but the tonnage is pretty well-fixed by the size of one's stomach. A major reason why the farmer has been in the dumps since the last war is that the demand for his output is less elastic than for manufactured goods. The very poor spend as much as half their income for food; the very rich spend only one or two per cent. If we were all millionaires, food consumption would no longer increase except as the population increased.

The same rough rule holds for medical care and for education through high school. It does not hold for houses or

1. E. H. Carr, *Conditions of Peace,* Macmillan, 1942, p. 89.

for clothes. The more income we have, the better houses we want and the nicer clothes. But even here there are limits. Most of us do not want to rattle around in a great palace with a lot of servants and eighteen bathrooms. That high ideal went out of fashion in 1929. You can pick up great palaces now at fire-sale prices, and no bidders. Most of us do not aspire to be smothered under piles of cotton underwear, wool sox, knickers and felt hats. Some clothing items, like food, have definite ceilings; others go on climbing with one's income—of which women's hats are an outstanding example. By and large the fixed wants are factory products, and the elastic wants are made to order, or produced by hand craftsmen.

In the United States we have seen many "luxuries" turn into "necessities" during the last two decades. When did they turn? When standardized quantity production took over the job. The outstanding example is the motorcar, but standardized men's suits, iceboxes, electric light and fixtures, radios, silk stockings (nylon is still more standardized), furniture "sets," fountain pens, kitchenware, all sorts of things, are now classed as mass comforts if not necessities, and have fallen out of the luxury class altogether.

In the chapters to come we shall emphasize basic wants. But mass comforts stand right behind them and will not be neglected. We shall be shooting at those articles which vary with population and not much with income. When they are manufactured articles, they are turned out by standardized methods of quantity production.

4
FOOD

HOW MUCH FOOD will be enough for the national family? We cannot calculate it simply in tons or carloads, because of certain complicated requirements. Instead of quoting from a textbook on nutrition, here is a story from Mexico to illustrate these complications.

For a thousand years and more, Aztec Indians on the Mexican plateau have eaten corn, beans and squash. Every spring the air is fragrant with the smoke of burning brush as the Indians prepare their milpas, with beans and squashes to be planted between the cornstalks. In addition to this basic diet, which supplies their bodies with the required energy, Aztecs have drunk a liquor called pulque, made from the century plant. A cavity is scraped out of the center of the huge heart with a machete, and sap drains into it from the ten-foot leaves. Sweetish, clear and colorless when drained, the sap is allowed to ferment into a milky fluid, smelling to high heaven, with an alcoholic content equivalent to that of strong beer. This the natives have drunk in vast quantities, man, woman and child. It was their favorite drink long before the Spaniards came in 1521.

A few years ago a prohibition movement got under way in

Mexico, and the government banned the making of pulque. This noble experiment had even more disastrous effects than our own. The Indians began to sicken all over the districts where pulque was banned. The medical problem was far worse than the police problem of handling a few village drunks. What was the answer to the mystery? It was solved by Dr. Jose Zozaya, one of Mexico's leading scientists. He analyzed pulque in the laboratory and found that it contained all the minerals and vitamins which the Indians were unable to obtain from an exclusive diet of corn, beans and squash! Pulque was an absolute essential to a balanced food supply. On the publication of these disclosures, the forces of prohibition retreated in disorder. Better to have citizens occasionally tipsy than chronically sick and dying. Pulque must remain until plateau Indians have access to its equivalent in such foods as oranges, green vegetables, milk.

Human beings outside of Mexico too must have various kinds of food if they are to keep healthy and survive. They need not only corn or its equivalent to give them energy, but also the juice of the century plant, or its equivalent. The body requires about forty different chemical substances regularly, some, like iron and calcium, in very small amounts. If any is long omitted, the penalties vary from that tired feeling to death. Scurvy, pellagra, rickets, are among the penalties. Primitive peoples knew nothing of science, but by trial and error they worked out diets which gave them the forty substances. They had to, or disappear from the face of the earth.

The "Gold Standard" of Nutrition

Thus the needs of our Great Family are two: an adequate quantity of energy-producing foods, something in the order of 2,000 to 3,000 calories a day for an adult, and a balanced diet which provides the forty essentials. One could get all the calories he needs from a quart of molasses a day, but he would not live long. The National Research Council recommends that you should get into your system every day on the average:[1]

Food energy	2,800	calories
Protein	66	grams
Calcium	0.9	grams
Iron	12	milligrams
Vitamin A	4,650	international units
Thiamin	1.5	milligrams
Ascorbic acid	70	milligrams
Riboflavin	2.2	milligrams

If you hand this list to a clerk in the A & P, he will probably call the police. But if you hand him the following list, he will treat you as entirely sane, and go about his business of filling it: milk, potatoes, beans, peas, nuts, tomatoes, oranges, grapefruit, lettuce, squash, apples, eggs, meat, chicken, fish, cereals, bread, butter, lard, sugar. You will need your sugar card for the last item. The essential substances may be had from other foods as well—pulque, for instance. The important point about a balanced diet is not to eat a rigid list of the same foods, but to be sure that all the important elements are included. Dr. Harris of the Massachusetts Institute of Technology has worked out a balanced ration which combines cereals, soybeans, peanuts, with minerals and vitamins, at a cost of only six cents a day. It weighs 1.5 pounds against the average daily food intake of 4.5

1. These essential nutrients have been translated into diets of everyday foods by the Bureau of Home Economics: "Planning Diets—by the New Yardstick of Good Nutrition," July 1941.

pounds. German soldiers use something like this ration in emergencies. You just add water, shut your eyes, and gulp it down. It will keep you healthy, or so it is claimed, but as a daily diet it would soon take all the joy out of living. What did the Lord give us a good appetite for? However, to starving Europeans at the present moment, Dr. Harris's ration would be a godsend.

Surgeon General Parran of the Public Health Service says that for the first time in history a "gold standard of nutrition" has been worked out. It has taken years of patient labor by many devoted scientists. It is based on the so-called protective foods, which have been so much publicized of late that most readers of this book are undoubtedly familiar with them, and full of health as a result of eating them.[2] What is less familiar is the idea of studying the diet and health of the nation as one great family. So long as we are making a food budget for this national family, we may as well plan for the kinds and proportions of foods which will feed us all adequately. If we set up as our standard the moderate-cost diet of the Bureau of Home Economics, we can calculate how much the Great Family needs of various foods in a year's time, and compare that with the family's actual consumption.[3]

The following table can be taken only as a rough indication, but with all due allowances, it tells a most important

2. A typical "gold standard" daily menu for an adult: one egg, one pint of milk, some meat, orange juice, one other fruit, two vegetables, one potato, three slices of bread, two tablespoons of butter.

3. Estimates of dietary shortages and overages vary from one investigator to another. The principal items, however, do not vary. I am giving a careful and conservative estimate made by the Resources Board, and the Bureau of Home Economics. Others have been prepared by Hazel K. Stiebeling, by Mr. McNutt's Federal Security Agency, and by practically all the home economics departments in the country. Consult your favorite household editor.

story about American food. Here are the figures:[4]

	Unit	Moderate Cost Diet Per Capita Requirements	Actual Consumption (1936-1940 Average)	Short	Over
Milk and milk products	Quarts	300	167	133	—
Leafy green and yellow vegetables	Pounds	166	73	93	—
Potatoes—including sweet	Pounds	155	149	6	—
Tomatoes and citrus fruits	Pounds	100	97	3	—
Meat, poultry, fish	Pounds	134	131	3	—
Eggs	Dozens	25	24	1	—
Beans, peas, nuts	Pounds	12	12	0	0
Other vegetables and fruits	Pounds	195	221	—	26
Sugars	Pounds	57	75	—	18
Fats	Pounds	57	67	—	10
Cereals and bread	Pounds	186	196	—	10

What we consume as a nation, however, is only a statistical average, and says little about what Smith eats or Jones eats. Perhaps Jones is a share cropper in Alabama and eats mostly hog and hominy. Perhaps Mrs. Smith is a 180-pound suburban, bridge-playing matron, and eats right down the list to the tune of three times the national average. If one man has an income of a million dollars and another has an income of a hundred dollars, their average income is $500,050, but that does not make the second man rich. The table shows what we are short of and long on, as a nation. It shows that all of us together do not consume as much food as we should to keep healthy. It indicates that, except for a large increase in dairy cattle, it would not be much of a trick to grow all the food we need. That is all it shows. Half the members of the family might be down with scurvy and rickets, while the

4. NRPB study, *Land Use Planning for Nutritional Needs,* March 1942. Figures adjusted to allow for children's diets.

other half might be fat as butter—but the table as it stands would never tell us so.

The Extent of Malnutrition

We must go to other sources to find the extent of undernourishment in the country. For instance, we go to reports of the Selective Service authorities and at once find something which hits us with a resounding thud: the percentage of young Americans deferred by draft physicians because of poor health. Approximately one candidate in two was rejected during the first year of Selective Service, though it must be remembered that standards were then higher than in the last war. Medical authorities agree that a great many of the rejections are due to poor food. The young man may not have had enough food, or, what is more probable, he has not had the right kinds of food.

Colonel R. A. Osmun of the Army Quartermaster Corps predicts a revolution in American food habits and farm production as a result of the diet which recruits in Army camps are now receiving. "Soldiers who lived at home on meat, potatoes and coffee, or on hominy grits, fat pork and molasses, are now learning what life is like with a balanced diet. Some of the men stick to meat and potatoes for the first few days in camp, but they soon begin wolfing down their carrots, lettuce, beans, peas and milk." Colonel Osmun reports a steady gain in weight and physique. "Our Army," he says, "is having one of the greatest experiences of our generation, the correct feeding of 2,000,000 men three times a day."[5]

Waldemar Kaempffert observes in *The New York Times* (May 3, 1942), that the American soldier is the best fed in

5. Reported in *The New York Times,* October 22, 1941.

the world. He gets more than 5,000 calories a day in a carefully balanced ration, and gains 8 to 16 pounds in a year. Well, if the American soldier why not the American people? There are plenty of us in slums and backward areas who would be better off with 8 to 16 more pounds of solid flesh. There are also some of us who would be better off with less solid flesh, and a proper diet brings that about too.

Paul V. McNutt, who as Federal Security Administrator ought to know, estimates that 75 per cent of all Americans need better diets, and 40 million are living below the diet danger line. Milo Perkins, who as inventor of the Food Stamp Plan also ought to know, estimated that, in 1939, 20 million Americans were living on an average of five cents worth of food per meal. By way of contrast, a boy in the armed services received about fifteen cents worth per meal.

In a nation-wide survey made in 1936, the Bureau of Home Economics found that only 27 per cent of American families had diets which could be rated as good; 38 per cent were classed as fair, and 35 per cent were definitely bad. Thirty-five per cent of 130 million works out to 45 million men, women and children inadequately nourished. A quarter of all farm families had bad diets, thus dispelling the myth about plenty to eat back on the old homestead. The average consumption of milk and green vegetables among children in families with incomes below $1,000, was *less than half* of what children consumed in families with incomes of over $2,500. "In place of these protective foods, the children ate more bread and potatoes." In the country today, according to the Department of Agriculture, there are upwards of 10 million children on deficient diets.[6]

6. *The School Lunch Program,* Bureau of Agricultural Economics, 1941.

In a recent Gallup poll (December 1941), half of all Americans interviewed—which is assumed to represent half the population—said they would like more to eat. The poll indicated that the typical family is consuming only half as much milk as the "gold standard" calls for. It also showed clearly that 50 per cent of U.S. adults have *not* learned the connection between diet and health. If our farmers began to produce the correct kinds and amounts of food tomorrow morning, they would be left with surpluses on their hands because many Americans do not yet know what the correct kinds and amounts are. A big task of education is in order. Mr. McNutt's office has produced a motion picture, called "Hidden Hunger," as one step in this education.

Among large groups of citizens education is well along. Long-term trends are in direction of better diets. Youngsters in college are taller, heavier, healthier, than their fathers and mothers were. The consumption of orange juice and vegetables is going up, while bread and cereals decline. The Food Stamp Plan has introduced grapefruit into many communities which had never before seen this admirable food. Even truck drivers are now eating salads and drinking milk without humiliation!

We have still a long way to go, however, to bring the low standard members up even to the moderate-cost diet level. When Mr. McNutt estimates that 75 per cent of all Americans are not properly fed, he does not mean the lower-income groups alone. The upper brackets also suffer from food deficiency, not because they do not have the money, but because they are ignorant or careless or unwilling to change their habits. Some of the worst undernourishment occurs on prosperous farms.

Making Good the Shortage

At any rate, we have to figure on providing our national family with the best diet we can and so we must pay serious attention to the proved shortages in essential items. What are the physical costs of making good the shortages? They are not great. Assuming that people become acquainted with dietetic standards in the next few years and are ready to eat on that basis, here are the changes needed in our food production.

Between 1936 and 1940, we devoted an average of 327 million acres to food production for domestic use. In 1950, to produce a balanced diet for 140 million people, we should need 336 million acres, *assuming no increase in yields per acre.*[7] Thus total cropland expands by only 2.5 per cent. But inside the grand total, important shifts must take place.

Wheat and other cereal crops should be reduced by 13 million acres.

Hay and feed grains should gain 21 million acres. (The hay is for the cows which produce the milk.)

Truck crops (for the leafy vegetables) should gain 2.8 million acres.

The hog, sheep and chicken population should increase somewhat. Milk cows should increase from 24 million to 32 million in 1950. Also a brisk upward movement in laying hens is indicated—from 369 million to 388 million.

The 1950 crop pattern requires that the wheat belts of the Great Plains and of the Pacific Northwest shift over in part to livestock and varied feed crops—incidentally reducing

7. Analysis by the Bureau of Agricultural Economics. The figure of 336 million acres in 1950 assumes a Spartan balanced diet for all Americans. If the upper-income groups continued to eat as well as they have in recent years, this figure would be raised considerably.

the dust-storm menace. The South should shift over in part from cotton to dairy farming, poultry, hay and pasture—incidentally reducing the menace of water erosion. The Bureau's 1950 pattern does not provide for food exports. In the late 1920's our food exports were grown on 51 million acres of cropland, which had shrunk to 30 million acres by the late 1930's. To feed parts of Europe and Asia after the war, a somewhat different pattern and larger acreage than that shown above will be required, temporarily at least.

The National Resources Planning Board sees no reason for an increase of man power on the farms. Indeed we can grow the "gold standard" in food for our own country with a smaller force than at present. The Bureau's estimates, furthermore, are based on average yields per acre in the late 1930's. It is highly probable that agricultural invention, stimulated as it will be by the war, will increase average yields. New fertilizers, new agricultural machinery, new strains, techniques of agrobiology, are constantly being introduced to improve efficiency.

As matters now stand, half our farmers receive only 12 per cent of all farm money income. This is the domain of the marginal farmers, the hillbillies, share croppers, tenant farmers, who barely earn a living, or depend in part upon government relief. Perhaps large numbers of them should leave their farms and go to work on other industrial fronts, where their contribution to the Budget can be more substantial. "Thus it is obvious," says the Resources Board, "that there is no rational basis for a recurrence of the back-to-the-land movement. . . . There is now a larger working population on the land than is needed to maintain normal production for a growing population."

The Board is statistically and economically correct. When the mechanical cotton picker and other laborsaving devices, now in the offing, descend on our fields, the need for labor per ton of crops will go down and down. But how about the need which untold millions of us feel to live on a patch of land rather than on a patch of asphalt? How about that, Mr. National Resources Planning Board? Remember how the characters of Steinbeck's *Of Mice and Men* yearned for a little cottage in the country where they could raise chickens. Farming is not only a business, it is perhaps even more a way of life. I doubt if anything can stop a back-to-the-land movement of citizens who want to raise chickens, vegetables, fruits for their own use, in connection with a paid job to which they commute.

Feeding Britain

Britain is now subsidizing[8] the production of flour, bread, meat, oatmeal, milk and other foods, in an attempt to keep the *whole population* well-nourished. The subsidy keeps prices to consumers low. Under pressure of bombers and submarines, the principle of a minimum Budget has been established in Britain.

Listen to R. M. Evans, head of the AAA, describing his trip to England in the fall of 1941:[9]

> Despite all the farmers of England are able to do for themselves, and despite all the rationing, the British say frankly: "Cut off American food tomorrow, and Great Britain is a thing of the past." . . . They showed us where the food is going, and their community feeding system. After the food is prepared at scattered points they put it in large thermos cans and rush it to the feeding centers where the

8. New York City has long used the subsidy method to keep subway rides at a nickel.

9. In *The Land,* Autumn 1941.

people get it—school children, and workingmen in the factory regions. These are the people who get it mostly. You can buy a meal at a community feeding center for 18 or 20 cents. If you prove that you haven't got the money, they'll give you the meal anyhow.

They really are giving the people all the food they can give them as cheaply as they possibly can. They are short of food; there isn't any question about that. Still, nobody is starving, but they don't have nearly enough of what they should have to do their best work. Said one Cabinet member: "You give us meat and we'll increase our production 20 per cent, just like that!"

Food is the hope of the hungry people of Europe. That is why food is going to play such a very important part when we get down to working out the peace. It will be the food America is producing that will provide tremendous power for building the kind of world free men can live in. . . .

I don't know how it will end, but when it ends every Englishman has agreed that postwar problems for them will be greater than war problems. . . . We talked a great deal about getting together on an all-out nutrition program to guarantee all people a decent diet as one of the ways in which America could use some of its agricultural surpluses. . . . No one knows what the peacetime world will be like, except that it will not be like anything we have ever known. I firmly believe it will be a world of opportunity—opportunity to build decent living standards for the many millions who have never known adequate food, clothing or housing. Those millions aren't all living in Europe. There are plenty of them in the United States. . . .

For the first time in history our agriculture is setting up a production schedule that consciously is taking into account reserves of food for freedom. My visit to Great Britain convinces me that these stock piles will be the biggest single factor in shaping the future course of world history.

British food controls have had very important effects on the United States. They are heading us in the direction of a sensible food budget for ourselves, by encouraging farmers to grow crops which contribute to a balanced diet. The encouragement comes through the stimulation of prices financed by Lend-Lease funds. The major products for Britain are dairy foods, especially dry skim milk, poultry, eggs, hogs, canned vegetables and fresh fruit. Skim milk is almost as loaded with vital elements as pulque. A farmer who gives cream to the children and skim to the pigs is doing better by his pigs than by his children.

Thus our crop pattern is definitely shifting under Lend-Lease pressure. It will shift more as the war goes on, and other Allies need our food. In 1942 we intend to send the British food that would fill a freight train 2,400 miles long. We intend to supply one-quarter of the food for the whole population! If these products are good for Londoners, why won't they be good for New Yorkers when the war and the shortages abroad are over? Why not hold the new crop pattern for our own requirements? Mr. Wickard has announced that this is precisely what he hopes to do. It is a striking example of how war necessities can be used in planning postwar adjustments.

The Food Stamp Plan is another step toward the Budget. Under its provisions some five million citizens are now receiving important elements of a balanced diet, while increasing their average food intake by 50 per cent, from 5 cents to 7.5 cents per meal. This brings them up to half what the boys in the Navy get. The School Lunch Plan is another step in the same direction. Some six million school children are receiving free at least one balanced meal a day. If the plan were doubled, every school child in the country who needed milk, fruit, vegetables, would be insured. When the President's proposal for proper feeding of young men rejected by the draft is put into mass action, another long step toward the Budget will be taken.

Summary of the Food Budget

Now let us gather the threads together and see what can be concluded about providing the Great Family with a "gold standard" of nutrition.

First, the standard has been worked out. Science has replaced guesswork. Individual differences and tastes will always play their part, but we know the forty chemical elements that the body must have.

Second, all authorities agree that a huge proportion of Americans are now short of receiving the standard. Perhaps 75 per cent are short to some degree, while at least 30 per cent—forty million persons—are living below the diet danger line. Shortages are due both to ignorance of the standard and to plain inability to buy the required foodstuffs.

Third, we have been growing almost enough food to meet the standard. However, the crop pattern must be shifted from wheat and cereals to more dairy products and vegetables. We have the plant, but it needs retooling in some departments.

Fourth, we do not need any more man power to meet the standard, now or in the future. Indeed, it would be better in the long run if there were fewer marginal farmers trying to scratch a living from rocky, leeched or eroded fields. Remember that our population is now growing relatively slowly, while scientific farming is growing very rapidly. A man has only one stomach.

A possible offset to this point is a bigger demand for non-food, or "technical," crops. Cotton is not too hopeful, but grain for alcohol and synthetic rubber, soybeans for plastics to be used in automobiles and airplanes, casein for synthetic wool, and the like, have great possibilities, and may keep more citizens on the soil than seems likely when we think of food production alone.

Fifth, the depression, and now the war, have forced Americans to think of themselves as one Great Family, and the government has taken long steps towards guaranteeing the Family's food supply. It will take more before the war is done. The Budget is squarely on the trend curve—not something which it would be nice to do someday. The rationing of sugar and other foodstuffs marks an important point on the curve. It indicates that *all* citizens are included, not just those who have the money to hoard a private supply.

Finally, we must not forget that, for a considerable period after the war, American farmers will have to feed the human family as well as the national family—or large sections of it in Europe, and perhaps in Asia and Africa as well. This will tend to give employment to farmers during the transition period, and ease the shock of demobilization.

A hundred years ago the Budget won out in the field of education after violent opposition. We now take it for granted that there should be a school desk for every child in the country. "If we can afford $100 a year to educate a child," says Vice President Wallace, "can't we afford $15 or $20 a year to keep that child physically fit for study?"

5
SHELTER

HOUSING IS A LARGE and cloudy term. It becomes concrete when you look hard enough at one particular house. I want to describe Uncle Henry's house in southeast Missouri. The description is not flattering, but I do not think Uncle Henry will greatly mind.

My guide, Hans Baasch, drove me along a rutted dirt road which ran east to the shore of the Mississippi River. The road led across the levee and over a plain dotted with pools of swamp water. On the higher ground cordwood was piled up, girdled trees were dying, and cotton was growing between the stumps. We went over a crazy bridge with a sign "Unsafe." "Well," said Hans, "we made it," and brought the car to a halt beside an unpainted shack in a wilderness of girdled stumps. It was Uncle Henry's place.

The house was perhaps eighteen feet square. It was set on wooden posts, two of which had quietly decomposed, giving the whole structure a distinct list to starboard. The roof of the porch had partially collapsed. A stovepipe jutted crazily out of a hole in the back wall. Beyond stood a foul privy with door askew and tar paper peeling off the roof.

Uncle Henry's rheumatism was so bad he could not get up

to welcome us. He sat in a broken-down armchair with springs coming out one way and stuffing the other. His eyes lit up when he saw Hans. While they talked I looked at Uncle Henry's house.

There were two rooms, the living-kitchen-dining room where we were, and one bedroom. Through a sagging door, I could see a cast-iron bed, a bureau, and a cracked mirror. There was no closet in either room.

The floor was of rough boards. It was a raw day and the wind was whistling through the cracks. Uncle Henry pulled the brown army blanket closer about him. "I don't feel good today," he said. Beside us was an iron stove with elaborate metal curlycues on the corners. It might once have belonged to some rich planter. It was cracked now and the pipe was smoking in time with the blasts of wind that came through the floor.

The walls of the rooms were made of unmatched vertical boards, insulated most ineffectively by pale-blue wrapping paper, peeling in long strips. Some repair work had been done with pages of the *St. Louis Post Dispatch.* I counted three broken panes in the two small windows. They were stuffed with old socks. In the corner stood an iron sink with a pail of water beside it; the pump was out in the yard. There was an old box half-full of firewood for the stove, a much-scrubbed wooden table holding an alarm clock and a year-old copy of the *Red Book;* a sewing machine, a shelf full of patent-medicine bottles; an insurance-company calendar, and a row of pegs hung with overalls, old coats and a battered hat.

When Hans had finished his business with Uncle Henry, we stood up to go. We both shook hands with the old man, shrunken in his blanket, his face grey with pain. "I guess I won't be here when you come next time, boy, but it was mighty nice to see you this time. And nice to see you, Mr. Chase."

"Oh, you're going to be all right," said Hans. "You're too tough to kill. You'll be chopping cotton again."

"Yes," said Uncle Henry, "I'm tough. You can't live here without being tough."

We had to drive up the road a bit before we could find a place to turn. I was mentally comparing Uncle Henry's cabin with the neat houses I had seen in the Farm Security project which Hans managed.

"Were all the houses like that when the government came in?" I asked.

"Some of them were worse," said Hans. "We took on a hundred families, and tore down ninety-four of the shacks. They were so rotten they hardly made decent firewood. Over three hundred kids were living in them. Up where I came from we wouldn't house a hog in such a place. We made an inventory of their furniture, clothes and tools. What do you suppose the average value was?"

"Judging from Uncle Henry's place, it couldn't have been much," I said.

"It was just twenty-eight dollars."

The Extent of the Housing Shortage

I liked Uncle Henry, but if I had to live in his house I would go out some dark night and jump in the Mississippi. I am not tough enough, and I doubt whether any human beings are really tough enough. But regardless of my personal opinion, when "housing" is discussed by learned statisticians, it is a good idea to have a clear picture in mind of Uncle Henry's house and others like it. A recent survey by the Department of Agriculture disclosed that at least 2,000,000 farmhouses are unfit for human habitation, while in Arkansas, Louisiana, Mississippi, Alabama and Georgia, the average value of farm dwellings is less than $500. It is also a good idea to think of the new houses in the project on the other side of the levee. We will come to them later.

In the meantime, let us go from Missouri cotton lands to a Massachusetts seaport. Learned statisticians and anthropologists from Harvard have been making an exhaustive survey of the town of Newburyport, at the mouth of the Merrimack River.[1] It used to be a shipping center and for a time it rivalled Boston. In that splendid era, captains and merchants built solid four-sided houses which make High Street perhaps the outstanding exhibit of colonial architecture in America. With the decline of shipping, Newburyport turned to the manufacture of textiles, boots and shoes, silverware. It never recovered its grandeur of sailing-ship days, but it never fell into such an economic backwater as did New Bedford and Fall River. Driving through, one gets an impression of a town housed above the average of New England towns. New England towns as a whole—perhaps due to a lack of economy in the use of white paint—give one the impression of being neater and in better repair than American towns generally.

The research staff from Harvard made a careful examination of the 12,424 houses in which the people of Newburyport lived. Here is what they found:

1. Warner and Lunt, *The Social Life of a Modern Community.* Investigators were in Newburyport for a number of years.

Houses in good repair	2,386 or 19 per cent of all
Houses in medium repair	4,938 or 40 per cent
Houses in bad repair	5,100 or 41 per cent

There were 403 large houses in good condition and 226 in bad condition. There were 1,107 medium-sized houses in good condition and 1,881 in bad. There were 876 small houses in good condition and 2,993 in bad. Well-to-do people lived mostly in the large houses, and poor people in the small houses, though the rule was not infallible.

From Newburyport we go to Washington, D. C. Within gunshot of the Capitol building you can find, if you know where to look for them, "Pork Steak Alley, Pig Alley, Goat Alley, Tin Can Alley, Coon's Alley, Tiger Alley, Moonshine Alley, Louse Alley and Chinch Row. These are Washington's Negro ghettos. Most of them are the back lots of the white residents of seventy years ago, and they were built to take care of the influx of refugee Negroes after the Civil War. The construction of alley dwellings was ended by law exactly fifty years ago, but most of the original shacks remain today. . . . The occupants of these alley shacks are a special brand of people, with their own customs, their own superstitions, and a notorious suspicion of outsiders. More than half the children born in the darkest alleys are illegitimate."[2]

The United States Census took an inventory of all the houses in the country, including Pork Steak Alley, Newburyport, and Uncle Henry's, in April 1940. The results speak for themselves.

There were then 37,327,000 dwelling units in the nation. This includes single houses, double houses counted as two, apartment houses counted for as many units as they contain.

2. W. M. Kiplinger, *Washington Is Like That,* Harper, 1942.

Almost half of all American houses (49.2 per cent) were in need of major repairs or had no bath, or both. There were 6,414,000 houses needing major repairs. Out of more than 7,000,000 farm units reported, 6,500,000 had no bath, 6,000,000 had no running water, only 31 per cent had electric current. Under the best of conditions many farm families will continue to use outside privies, employ pumps instead of running water, and in lonely areas forego electric current. But any way you look at them the Census figures indicate a dreadful shortage of adequate shelter on the farms and in the cities. One does not need statistics to prove this, one only needs a pair of eyes.

In Arkansas there were 521,000 houses, according to the 1940 Census. Twenty-two thousand had one room, 90,000 had two rooms, 3,500 had ten rooms or more. Twenty-six per cent of all had four rooms; 46 per cent had less than four; only 28 per cent had more than four rooms. Arkansas is one of the states which is in direst need of adequate shelter.

Let us compare equipment in Georgia, Tennessee and Oregon, again using Census figures:

	Georgia	*Tennessee*	*Oregon*
Number of houses with electric light	46.6%	50.9%	85.8%
With mechanical refrigeration	24.7	27.7	43.4
With no refrigeration	45.6	44.5	47.8
With no central heating	93.1	86.7	65.2
With a radio	52.5	62.5	89.5

In houses with no refrigeration a large amount of food is likely to spoil. In the south, refrigeration is especially needed to keep the family healthy. Houses with no central heating may do in many southern areas, but not so well in Oregon. Houses without radios are liabilities in a total war, where citizens need instant communication.

A Ten-Year Budget for Shelter

The Census gives a dramatic picture of the vast task before the country in the department of shelter. To provide decent houses for all members of the Great Family cannot be done in any one year, but calls for a program stretching over a decade or more. There is no way to tell from these figures, or from any other figures, exactly how many homes need to be demolished as unfit for human habitation, how many need to be renovated from the foundations, how many can be salvaged by major repairs.

Various estimates have been made, however, of the total number of new units needed in the years before us to bring housing up to par. Miss Catherine Bauer, a noted expert in the field, estimated that between 1937 and 1950, sixteen million units ought to be built to care for the increase in families, and to replace the worst of the substandard structures. Mrs. Edith Elmer Wood, another recognized authority, estimated in 1938 that some 13 million units, not including farmhouses, should be built by 1950. This checks roughly with Miss Bauer's calculations. Both indicate a building program of more than 1,000,000 units a year. The best year we ever had, 1925, accounted for 900,000 new houses. In 1933, the number was down to 93,000. By 1940 it had climbed to 600,000.

Mr. C. F. Palmer, Federal Housing Co-ordinator, told a Fortune Round Table in the summer of 1941 that after the war we should build 1,600,000 nonfarm units annually for ten years, to house the urban population properly. He thinks that private finance can swing a million of them, but that government subsidy will be required for 600,000 units a year. For the ten-year period, this would mean 6 million units subsidized for low-income families. Mr. Palmer reminds us that European governments, in the years before the war, subsidized 20 million urban units.

I think we can take it as demonstrated that the Budget will call for somewhere between a million and two million dwelling units, over the whole country, every year, for at least ten years after the war ends. That will make the biggest single demand upon man power of any project on the horizon—the largest pool for postwar work. According to Mr. Palmer, it will keep at least 1,600,000 construction workers busy; a high government source estimates 2,000,000 workers. It may mean two to three times the labor force which was building houses in 1940, when 600,000 units were constructed.

These estimates do not include labor for lumber and other materials, but only men on the job. On the average, it looks as if one man puts up one house in a year's time. When prefabrication goes into mass production, it is probable that a house can be put up in a far shorter time, say a man month, or a man fortnight—the latter being the equivalent of a crew of seven putting the house up in two days. And although the factory cost of the prefabricated units will be greater than the factory cost of the lumber, nails, paint and other materials used at present—measured in man hours, or dollars, or any way you please—the total man power required to meet the housing budget will be less than under prewar conditions. By early 1942, the government had ordered 22,058 "demountable" or prefabricated houses for war workers.[3] One San Francisco firm alone was given a contract for 5,000, the largest order for prefabrication ever placed!

3. News release from the Federal Works Agency, February 1942.

Our Most Backward Industry

The residential construction industry, as at present organized is, to quote Dr. Alvin H. Hansen and Guy Greer, "our most backward industry. In an age of mass production and assembly lines, it remains today, with a few noteworthy exceptions, a small-scale handicraft business which hardly deserves to be called an industry at all. It is made up of large numbers of contractors, subcontractors, material dealers, trade-unions, and so on. And, in spite of numerous honest carpenter builders and a few larger operators, it is shot through and through with graft, rackets and conspiracies. Topping all this, the manufacture of several important building materials and of much equipment is a virtual monopoly. The result is that every kind of dwelling costs far too much, even while the so-called industry is not, and has not been, prosperous for many years."[4] Establishing our Budget might not only give us adequate houses, but conceivably it might clean up an Augean stable as well. No labor group has suffered more severely from unemployment than workers in the building trades, and few have suffered more from racketeering officials.

One reason why the construction industry is in such a deplorable state may be that it has been tied all along to the cart of land speculation. The men who have put up the money, by and large, have not been interested in houses for people to live in. They have been interested in developing property as an investment, or, as it has been described, in "buying by the acre and selling by the front foot." Now, with the prospect of population gradually levelling off, and

4. *Urban Redevelopment and Housing,* National Planning Association, Pamphlet No. 10, December 1941.

real-estate values practically stationary from the same cause, we have a chance for the first time in our history to create a really efficient construction industry. No trouble is foreseen in finding the man power, the materials and the skills to build 1,500,000 houses, or 2,000,000 houses per year, after the war. We built almost 900,000 urban units in 1925, under handicraft, racket-ridden methods. If the industry could be rationalized, its capacity would be greatly increased.

Defining Adequate Shelter

We have been talking about "houses," and "dwelling units." A better term for this department of the Budget is "shelter." Shelter can be defined as not only the floor, walls and roof of a house, but the land on which it stands, the furnishings and equipment inside it, and the services running into it—water, electricity, gas, telephone, waste disposal.

The first requisite of adequate shelter is a place where children can be reared in health and well-being. The child is my test of shelter. Will this house help his development or set it back? In such a test, the question of how many ice cubes the refrigerator can produce, or whether a Colonial design is to be preferred to a straight-line international job, sinks into insignificance. The province of the Budget is to give children and their parents a clean, healthy place to live in, not to help them keep up with the Joneses. On this standard, the size and construction varies with the size of the family and with the climate. A winter home in Maine must be a more solid affair than a winter home in Florida.

Allowing for the climatic differences over our great continent, a set of rough specifications for adequate shelter might read something like this:

A tight, honestly built structure, of reasonably good design, which can be kept adequately clean and warmed in winter.

Space enough for children to play. In city apartments this can be solved to a degree by playgrounds between the blocks. Land to grow flowers or vegetables or both, wherever possible.

Minimum equipment for sanitation, to include pure water, bathing facilities, screens, toilet facilities. For the latter, sanitary privies may be acceptable in some rural areas. In cities, flush toilets connected with the sewer system are mandatory for reasons of public health.

Electric lighting and refrigeration in most cases, and for most families a telephone.

Simple and substantial furnishings. There may be a great future for metal furniture after the war, to make use of our vast aluminum supply and bomber plants.

Farmhouses at LaForge

When Hans and I got back to the Farm Security project at LaForge, I had a chance to see with my own eyes the kind of shelter I have been trying to outline above. Here were one hundred well-designed farm cottages on 5,000 acres of farmland. Sixty of them were occupied by white people and forty by Negroes, but there was no way of telling from the outside which house belonged to which. After the government bought the land in 1937 and decided to "resettle" the 100 share croppers then living on it, its first task was to dismantle the shacks and build some real shelter. Listen carefully to the way in which this task was accomplished. It may carry important suggestions for the postwar Budget.

Remembering certain sad experiences from rural resettlement projects in the past, where members were provided with electric refrigerators and flush toilets but no visible means of support, engineers of the Farm Security Administration designed a very modest house. They went into action and built 94 new houses in 100 days, at an average cost of $1,100 per house, a cost which fitted the return from the land. The whole project now comes close to paying its way. The FSA did it by an ingenious method of mass production, in which the project members did most of the work. Lumber was unloaded from freight cars in a field near the cotton gin. It was cut into standard sizes with power saws. The units were then nailed into sections—walls, roof trusses, partitions. The sections were loaded into trucks and taken to the site, where concrete posts had already been set up by another crew of LaForge men. In half a day or so the house was up, in another day or two it was painted. One day, on a bet, a crew put a house up in thirty minutes. A few skilled supervisors and carpenters kept the job moving on schedule.

We enter one of the houses, going through a screened porch into a good-sized living room with screened windows —which work—and a double floor. The walls are vertical tongue-and-groove stock, well-oiled, in natural wood. Furniture includes a stove for heating, a couch, chairs, a big table, a carpet, curtains at the windows. The kitchen beyond has an enameled sink but no running water. It has built-in cabinets, and a substantial cookstove, burning wood or coal. Wood may be had for the cutting, over beyond the levee. Electric current is in every house, but used mostly for lighting. Two bedrooms—in some cases three—open from the living room. The bedrooms have closets, double beds, a dresser, mirror and chairs. The cold north wind was still blowing, but every house I visited was snug, warm and clean. They lacked frills and gadgets but they did not lack cheer, in spite of getting down to the bare essentials of shelter in that climate.

Outside in the yard is a sealed well with pump, and, in the far corner, a sanitary privy. An earth-covered root cellar, full of homemade preserves and canned goods, and a small, well-built barn, complete the property. In the North, construction would have to be somewhat heavier, but beyond this I cannot conceive of a fairer, sounder minimum standard of rural shelter than this LaForge project. To come into it from Uncle Henry's place is to come from hell into heaven. If a hundred such units can be constructed by the people who are to live in them, why not a million?

New Structural Principles

The present government program for war workers calls for 670,000 housing units. The urgent need of war housing is well illustrated in Ford's new bomber plant at Willow Run, Michigan. Seventy thousand workers are needed to roll out the bombers. "There are virtually no houses near the plant and it is almost impossible to rent a home in Detroit, 25 miles away."[5] Nor will gasoline rationing help the situation.

As a result of these urgencies and stringencies, the construction industry, both public and private, is being rushed into an era of experimentation which may have great and enduring results after the war. "For the first time in our history," writes Douglass Haskell, "we are introducing a whole series of new structural principles into common houses. They

5. *Time,* May 5, 1942.

come over from airplanes, ships, planetaria, bridges."[6] Here, for instance, is a prefabricated home made of plywood in which structural strength depends not on orthodox joists, beams and rafters, but on a light frame with a plywood skin. It allows the greatest freedom in placing of doors, partitions and windows. Here is a "tailored to order" apartment house being worked out by Walter B. Sanders for the Revere Copper and Brass Company. It will have prefabricated wall panels, permitting each tenant to have the number of rooms, closets, cupboards and windows he finds most convenient, and then to change the arrangement from summer to winter, or when Aunt Hattie comes for a long visit. "This is all 100 per cent possible today," says Mr. Sanders. "Elements to build such an apartment house are now in mass production—columns, beams, wall panels, floor panels, partitions and pipes."[7]

One great barrier against prefabrication has been the building-trade unions. Naturally they do not want to lose their jobs to a factory. But Mr. Haskell believes that the CIO has seen the handwriting on the wall. In Sweden, trade-unions withdrew their opposition to factory-built houses when they realized that only mass production could supply needed shelter for all workers. Let Mr. Haskell, an architect and a profound student of the subject, have the final word:

> Prophecies are hard to make at a time like this, but it would appear that the badly needed industrialization of building has been definitely put under way. . . . The nation that won its fame building skyscrapers is at work again, but the job of building everybody a decent place to live in is a far broader and worthier aim.

6. "The Revolution in House-Building," *Harpers,* June 1942.
7. Associated Press report, March 26, 1942.

6

CLOTHING

NO "GOLD STANDARD" has been proposed for clothing, as it has for nutrition. There could hardly be one, because the human body was not designed to wear clothes. Nature makes no demands for shirts and socks. Clothing becomes mandatory only for certain special purposes—three purposes, in fact:

To protect the body against cold, when *homo sapiens* moves out of his "natural" climate.

To protect the body against injury or infection in performing certain kinds of work. Such clothing as overalls, gloves, leather aprons, boots, helmets, meet this purpose.

To protect the mind against criticism, if the folklore of the tribe prescribes clothes. All civilized tribes prescribe clothes except in bathtubs, whatever the temperature. A citizen without clothes suffers more mental anguish than a citizen without food.

The minimum requirements seem to be enough clothing to keep one warm, enough to protect against injury in daily tasks, and enough to make every member feel unashamed in the presence of his fellows. These requirements do not present a great problem.

The Extent of Clothing Shortages

In 1939, estimates made by a federal government agency showed that if everyone in the country could buy as much clothing as a family living on an income of $1,800 a year now buys, production would have to be raised about 10 per cent. Families on $1,800 a year do not have many mink coats or white ties. That level, however, represents a minimum standard of health and decency at 1939 prices. The agency estimated that a 10 per cent increase would give jobs to about 250,000 people.

The most complete analysis of the clothing budget ever made to my knowledge is that of the National Survey of Potential Product Capacity, referred to in Chapter 1. Taking the year 1929 as the base, the Survey listed the quantities of suits, coats, shoes, hats, underwear, and other major items actually produced. It then estimated how many of these articles could have been produced if all textile mills and garment shops had been operating at capacity. Finally, it proceeded to dress the Great Family in what it considered adequate garments, and see what those totals amounted to. Take shoes, for instance:

We actually produced in 1929	361 million pairs
We could have produced	550 million pairs
But we needed only	395 million pairs

When all the major items were priced in 1929 dollars, the following extraordinary picture came to light:

Total value of major items of clothing produced	$ 7,800,000,000
Total value of capacity production	$16,777,000,000
Total value of adequate production for the Budget	$12,196,000,000

So we had the cotton, wool, hides, findings, tanneries,

textile mills, shoe and hat factories, garment factories, to produce *more than twice as much clothing* as was actually turned out. But we could hardly have used any such Niagara of suits, pajamas, sweaters, dresses, pants, shirts and overalls. Citizens would have looked like the White Knight going into battle, padded into immobility. We could have used, however, more than we got by about 56 per cent. The women of the country got 206 million frocks during the year and could have used 275 million; they got 615 million pairs of stockings and could have used 681 million; men got 9 million overcoats and could have used 36 million—which means roughly an overcoat every other year.

The National Survey went higher up the scale than the 1939 government study. It included not only bare essentials but all factory-made clothing, whether designed for protection or for conspicuous consumption. It did *not* include custom-made clothing, where, of course, conspicuous consumption reaches its peak. It said nothing whatever about quality, but dressed folks in what was actually being bought in 1929.

Since that year we have had the ebb and flow of styles as usual, but our clothing requirements have not changed a great deal, nor has the clothing industry. We have more and better American designers. Manufacturers of sportswear have increased. Synthetic fabrics have been improved and their production has grown substantially. Most citizens probably possess a more varied wardrobe than they used to, especially in sport clothing.

Nevertheless, I think the increase of 56 per cent, which the Survey recommended, is too high. I think the Great Family could get along comfortably with something less than that, especially if quality were improved so that shoes and overcoats would wear longer. But the National Survey brings out two points of the highest importance for our study.

It proves beyond all doubt that the American clothing industry, from cotton in the fields to garment shops on Seventh Avenue, New York, has been entirely capable for more than thirteen years of turning out more than we can conveniently wear.

It proves further that mass-produced clothing has a fairly definite limit, though less definite than the limit in food. Both tend to vary with the population, as was pointed out earlier. The market for neither essential is indefinitely expansible, in spite of the best efforts of fashion institutes to pyramid the demand.

Well, you ask, if we can use only a limited amount of clothing, how can the daughter of a great tycoon travel with sixteen trunks and spend $150,000 a year on frocks alone? That's easy. Because the Princess de la Palusa carries, say, $50 worth of factory-produced clothes in those trunks, while all the rest is hand-made, custom-built, French-couturière stuff. If we are going into this department, the Princess is a piker compared with many an Indian rajah. He may have a hat coated with rubies valued at $5,000,000. We are talking about clothes for the folks.

Clothing the Army

The enormous capacity of the clothing and textile industries may be fully used, for once, in outfitting the armed forces this year. Purchases have been so extensive that a group of businessmen—presumably merchants who sell clothes to civilians—has charged the Army with overbuying. These businessmen say that there need be no shortage of clothing for the rest of us if the Army bought only what it needed.[1] But it is buying clothes enough to dress the entire male population from 16 to 64! With more wool, for instance, being ordered for uniforms and Army blankets than the entire population normally uses in a year, civilians must naturally get along with less.

The Army retorts that soldiers wear out boots and uniforms very fast, and that extra supplies have to be available both at home and in foreign bases. Perhaps this means that heavy stores of equipment are being sent to Australia and Iceland and Egypt and North Ireland and many other places; stores for more troops than may ever be sent to wear them. But we civilians will hardly grudge them their outfits, worn or unworn.

Far from complaining with the businessmen about the shortages in civilian attire, I am inclined to think that they may prove, as the dietitians say of the sugar rations, a blessing in disguise. They will not be any blessing if the government policy is to allow us the usual number of garments and skimp on each garment, but only if the policy is to improve *quality* so that fewer replacements are required. If we civilians, with more money than usual to spend in adorning our persons, must walk the streets in suits of shoddy wool, collarless and bursting at the seams, we shall be wanting to replace those suits at the first opportunity. But if we can get a good-quality, long-wearing suit and at the same time be relieved of sales pressure to buy a newer style three months later, we may be glad to wear that suit some months longer and buy more War Bonds with what we save.

1. *The New York Times,* June 7, 1942.

Uniforms by Hartnell

The British, after two and a half years of war, with clothing rigidly rationed for a good part of that time, have a new plan for women's clothes that will save labor and materials while dressing the average Englishwoman better than she has ever been dressed before. The plan involves a certain amount of standardization, a great improvement in quality, and low prices for styles devised by the best designers in London. Norman Hartnell, dressmaker to the Queen, and a few other designers, are producing perhaps thirty models, to be made in a variety of sizes and colors, of durable fabrics, with careful tailoring and reinforced seams. The file clerk in a factory office will part with a few coupons from her ration book and twenty or thirty shillings, and go proudly to work wearing a Hartnell model in which she will look smart for several seasons.

A similar program in this country, by reducing the heavy turnover in short-wearing clothes, would release many bolts of cloth to be made into extra uniforms in case the soldiers need them. It would educate consumers to wear clothes of better quality, though of limited variety. After the war they could express their personalities again in a greater number of styles, but they would still insist on that fine old wartime workmanship. Some quantity producers and some merchants might not get back all their business, but the uniform manufacturers can hardly equal their war production in peacetime, whatever happens. They will come closer to capacity, if a budget of clothing is made available to all citizens, than they have ever come in peacetime.

Clothing is one of the Big-Five essential requirements, and a minimum standard is important, in quality as well as quantity. But in contrast with food, shelter or health service, the problem of meeting this minimum is relatively simple. When a poor Russian immigrant girl arrived in New York a generation ago, she thought that the whole population was composed of counts and countesses. As compared with the population of Moscow or Kiev, their clothes were resplendent. If she had landed on an Alabama farm her reaction would have been different.

7

HEALTH

OF THE FIRST two million men examined for the Army in 1940-1941, almost one million were rejected because their physical condition was below Army standards. These were men supposedly in the healthiest years of their life, in a great rich country which spends many millions for doctors, medicines, hospitals, and advertisements about health and sanitation. Yet half of these young men were not physically fit for Army work. We do not need any more facts or figures than this to prove that the Great Family is in grave need of better medical care. A large number of the rejections, as we noted earlier, were due to inadequate diet. Some were due to congenital ailments—beyond the power of medical science to cure. But a large fraction can be laid squarely to insufficient medical, dental, clinical, hospital and public-health attention.

The Extent of Ill-Health

Let us take the lowest third of our population, often mentioned by President Roosevelt. It comprises more than forty million citizens. These citizens in an average year will have eight million cases of sickness serious enough to lay them up for more than one week. In two million cases they will receive no medical attention at all. Meanwhile, among persons who were on relief, disabling illnesses in 1935 were 62 per cent more frequent than in the highest income groups.[1]

In an average year 225,000 American women will give birth to children without the help of a doctor. Only 25 per cent of rural births take place in hospitals; in cities the ratio is 84 per cent. Two-thirds of all rural communities lack child-health centers. Of the 75,000 stillbirths a year, it is estimated that about 30,000 could be saved by better medical attention. Of the 70,000 babies dying in their first month, half could be saved. Each year 100,000 Americans die from pneumonia, 62,000 from tuberculosis—rates altogether too high. The new "sulpha" drugs make it possible to reduce pneumonia deaths greatly, but only a few states have yet set up effective programs for using them. More than 70 per cent of our industrial workers are employed in small factories (under one hundred employees) where industrial hygiene services are inadequate or altogether absent.[2]

The National Institute of Health reported that in 1935-1936 persons on relief averaged 17.4 days of illness a year; persons not on relief but with family incomes of under $1,000 averaged 10.9 days of illness; persons in the $1,500 to $2,000 a year income group averaged 7.0 days; persons with incomes of over $5,000, 6.5 days of illness. Here is a stunning statistical parallel between poverty and sickness. Adequate medical care for the lower-income groups would not, of course, completely close the gap. Some of the individuals are poor because they are sick, not the other way

1. *Proceedings* of the National Health Conference, July 1938.
2. Public Health Bulletin No. 259, 1940.

around. But even with these, there is a vicious circle in which citizens grow sicker and poorer. Illness results not only from lack of doctors and hospitals, but from lack of good food, good shelter, warm clothing, adequate education. In the last analysis, the Big Five are all tied together.

In 1940 the Farm Security Administration made a study of 2,500 families in twenty-one rural counties in seventeen states, as a kind of Gallup poll sample of health on the farm. More than 11,000 individuals were included. Sixty-nine per cent of them had unfilled cavities in their teeth. Seventy-nine per cent of all white persons had impaired hearing, and 55 per cent defective tonsils. Twenty-six per cent of the children under fifteen had defective vision in both eyes. About 3 per cent of white children and 6 per cent of colored children had rickets. Meanwhile the Public Health Service has estimated that a family needs to spend at least $60 a year to receive minimum medical care. If this is true, some four million farm families, with net cash incomes of under $1,000, cannot meet the standard.

It is said that in large cities, at least, only the very rich and the very poor have their health properly attended to. The rich can pay their doctors, while the poor are not too proud to go to free clinics. The great middle classes take it on the chin. Outside of the larger cities the opportunities for free services are generally severely limited.

Not Enough Doctors

There is no "gold standard" for medical care, any more than there is for clothing. It is possible to estimate the number of doctors, dentists, nurses, hospital beds needed to give a stated number of Americans adequate medical attention.

The Committee on the Costs of Medical Care has provided data for such estimates.[3] Their figures are based on the year 1929. In that year 179 dentists were needed to take care of the teeth of a community of 100,000, but only 56 were available, on the average. No wonder so many draftees were rejected because of bad teeth. In 1929, 142 doctors were needed for 100,000, and 126 were in attendance. In many areas the shortage was far greater than the national average. In the same year, 460,000 more hospital beds should have been available for the Great Family as a whole, together with many more nurses and lay hospital personnel to take care of the patients.

In 1937, the Technical Committee on Medical Care reported to the National Health Conference that there were 4,500 general hospitals in the country, with 410,000 beds. Two counties out of five did not have a registered general hospital, and in many farm communities the only hospitals within striking radius were small institutions of low standards. The Committee estimated that we needed a total of 180,000 beds in general hospitals alone, some to be added to existing hospitals, the majority to be provided by the construction of 500 new hospitals. We also needed 500 rural health and diagnostic clinics. We needed 50,000 more beds for tuberculosis patients, and 130,000 more beds for mental patients. The PWA has built many hospitals since 1937, and the situation is better today.

The Committee on the Costs of Medical Care estimated that more than a million persons were engaged in what might be called the "health industries," at a total dollar cost

3. Roger I. Lee and Lewis W. Jones, *The Fundamentals of Good Medical Care,* University of Chicago Press, 1933.

of about $3.5 billions a year. To inaugurate Budget standards would not raise the present man-power total much. As in the case of the Budget for food, some drastic *internal* shifts would be necessary. Quacks would give way to certified medical men. Patent nostrums would give way to scientific drugs. The professional staff, however, would be obliged to work full time to meet the national need, where now it is often on part time. One way of doing this would be through group-medicine programs where citizens themselves organize their own hospital and medical services. The effects of such a reorganization would be twofold—more income for doctors, dentists and nurses; more medical care for the population.

If we had not gone to war and could make plans under normal conditions, we should not be far wrong, I think, if we assumed that with all due allowance for internal adjustments, the Budget required an increase of one third in total professional personnel. Dentists would be over this figure; doctors under it. Hospitals would need to be further expanded, and large increases would be needed in public health facilities. Full-time local health officers are urgently required in rural districts, and more effective work for controlling communicable diseases, like malaria, syphilis, gonorrhea, tuberculosis, pneumonia, also more work for controlling cancer. These increases, it goes without saying, should not be bunched in upper-bracket communities as health facilities now tend to be. They should be spread over the nation, especially in farm areas.

What the War is Doing to the Medical Services

Now that we are at war, however, the picture is even more

complicated. The war is turning the health industries upside down. Many thousands of doctors, dentists and nurses have been taken out of ordinary practice and inducted into the armed services. All medical men in the country have been required to fill out a questionnaire stating their training, experience and specialties. "For many of them it forecast an end of the old competitive practice of private medicine. The questionnaire made it clear to the doctors that they would have to co-operate in some form of organized medical service."[4] They were asked to choose among four alternatives: to accept commissions in the Army, the Navy, to work for the Public Health Service, or to accept assignments in such federal agencies as the Indian Service, Veterans Administration, Panama Canal Zone, Children's Bureau.

> Before the war is over, it may well be that more than 50,000 doctors (out of a total present personnel of about 160,000) will be on full-time salaries from our government. . . . This number is in addition to the 20,000 on government salary before Hitler invaded Poland. . . . How will these 50,000 be demobilized when war ends? Some of them will never have had private practice; most of the others, after several years of war, will have lost the private connections they once had. How far will the government have to go in organizing and financing a start for doctors in civilian life?[5]

New munitions factories are springing up in areas where a year ago medical facilities were geared to half or a quarter of the present population. Meanwhile there is a whole new accent on the value of man power. It is no longer a drug on the market. Skilled labor is an especially precious national asset. The "human machines" must be kept at the highest efficiency if we are to win the war. Suddenly on our door-

4. *Time,* May 11, 1942.
5. Dr. Michael M. Davis in *The New Republic,* June 1, 1942.

step we find a vast medical problem of maintaining the health of war workers, out of which may come new techniques for maintaining the health of the whole population.

Right beside this is another vast medical problem: to rehabilitate young men rejected by the draft, where defects are remediable. Right behind it is the vast medical problem of caring for wounded and handicapped soldiers and sailors discharged from the armed services. The chief dental officer of the Selective Service System said, in May 1942, that the greatest medical, dental and surgical rehabilitation program in United States history was under way. He said that the dental profession was about to start work on the teeth of 200,000 young men rejected by draft boards. Extractions, fillings, dentures, will be provided at the expense of the government. The patient can go either to a private dentist or to an Army dentist. A similar program will apply to registrants who need emergency surgical or medical repair.

While the long-range problems of the Budget stand, a short-term health program for war is right on top of us. It promises to loosen up the medical profession, both physically and mentally, as nothing else could. Medical men may have to be rationed like sugar—so many for the armed services, so many for the war industries, so many for the public-health services of the government, the balance for the civilian population. When doctors are reduced in number on any given front, there is greater need that their services shall be efficiently used, economizing time and skill and ending various wasteful practices of competition. As Dr. Michael M. Davis says, a whole new philosophy of medical care may come out of this war program. The wartime health budget may pave the road for the peacetime budget.

Group Medicine

It does not follow that the government needs to run the mechanics of meeting the Budget. Group medicine has already made important headway. I belong, for instance, to a group hospital plan, whereby I pay some $20 a year and any member of my family can go to the hospital free for two weeks, and have reduced rates for longer treatment. The same practice can be applied to doctors' services. Health insurance, health co-operatives, can be organized by citizens themselves, and many programs are being so organized. The more we can do the job ourselves the less the need for the government to do it. The government, however, should make sure that in some form or other *every citizen has access to the service.* Meanwhile, every improvement in diet, housing and education will raise the general level of public health.

People fail to go to doctors either because they cannot afford to, or because they are ignorant. To achieve the goal of minimum health services, it will not only be necessary to remove the first reason by making medical care available to all, but to provide a great deal of education as well. If this means a flank attack on the vested rights of the patent-nostrum industry, sometimes known as the pain and beauty boys, the public may be able to face it with fortitude.

8

EDUCATION

NO FLANK ATTACKS would be needed to establish a national minimum Budget for education. No vested interests remain to oppose the Budget here. They were liquidated a hundred years and more ago. Free universal public education is the accepted rule, not only in America but throughout western civilization. It was not won, however, without a fight.

> A great struggle for the creation of a series of tax-supported, publicly controlled and directed, and nonsectarian common schools was in progress. . . . Excepting the battle for the abolition of slavery, perhaps no question has ever been before the American people for settlement which has caused so much feeling or aroused such bitter antagonisms. To meet the arguments of the objectors . . . to overcome prejudice . . . was the work of a generation.[1]

Education is now solidly in the Budget, after a struggle which was only less violent than the struggle against slavery. If education, why not food, shelter, health and clothing? Because we have never thought about the other four in the same way. The war is forcing us to think about them now. The postwar adjustment will make us think about them even

1. Ellwood P. Cubberley in the *Encyclopaedia Britannica.*

harder, when the mass demands for security will be paralleled by a demand for jobs. The Budget can furnish millions of jobs, as we have seen. The fact that universal education is already accepted without opposition provides advocates of the Budget a strong advance position.

In 1807 there was no such advance position. Listen to the President of the Royal Society in England, testifying on a bill in Parliament to provide free elementary schools: "However specious in theory the project might be of giving education to the laboring classes and the poor, it would in effect be found to be prejudicial to their morals and happiness . . . it would enable them to read seditious pamphlets, vicious books, and publications against Christianity; it would render them insolent to their superiors. . . ."[2]

Because public schools are operated by the government, with teachers on the public pay roll, and revenues drawn from taxes, it does not follow that food, shelter, clothing and health services should be so operated. It only follows that all the Big Five should be in what Geoffrey Crowther called the domain of "order," or as lawyers phrase it, "affected with a public interest." It should be the duty of community planning authorities to see to it that all citizens receive their minimum quota. That does not mean manufacturing it for them; it means making sure that the output, which private business largely produces, *gets to them.* It is a steering and planning job.

If the government through its monetary and fiscal controls insures a high level of national income and of employment, citizens themselves will be able to buy the bulk of their essentials without any planning at all. Market demand will

2. Quoted by J. L. and Barbara Hammond in *The Town Laborer.*

take care of it. It is only where this automatic system fails to cover certain groups of citizens that the government needs to exert direct controls. The most obvious case is that of shelter, where it has been clearly demonstrated that private enterprise simply cannot afford to supply adequate housing for people in the lower-income groups.

The Extent of the Shortages in Education

Education is accepted in the domain of order, but a serious shortage still remains to be overcome before all American children receive their due quota. Floyd B. Reeves of the American Youth Commission estimates that to give every normal child education through high school or its equivalent would require more than a 60-per cent increase in the teaching staff of the country.[3] To meet Mr. Reeves's standard 1,650,000 teachers would be needed; we have today something over 1,000,000.

A quarter of a million men, physically fit, have been rejected by draft boards because of illiteracy, lack of education, low mentality. The largest group were neither aliens nor Negroes but native whites. Georgia, Louisiana, Mississippi and South Carolina had the worst records. Huey Long's strength was in this area.

The 1940 Census pictured the present educational situation of our adult population. It asked everybody in the country twenty-five years of age and over how much schooling he had had. Here are the answers:

	Number of Persons	*Per Cent*
No schooling at all	2,800,000	3.7
1 to 4 years of grade school only	7,305,000	9.8
5 to 8 years of grade school	34,413,000	46.0

3. *Journal of Educational Sociology,* October 1941.

	Number of Persons	*Per Cent*
1 to 3 years of high school	11,182,000	15.0
4 years of high school	10,552,000	14.1
1 to 3 years of college	4,075,000	5.4
4 years of college or more	3,407,000	4.6
Unknown	1,042,000	1.4
Total persons more than 25 years old	74,776,000	100.0

Of all Americans 25 years of age or over, almost 60 per cent have never gone beyond grade school; more than 13 per cent have never gone beyond the fourth grade, and almost 4 per cent have never gone to school at all. How many good potential doctors, scientists, businessmen, poets, administrators, mathematicians, fighting pilots, artists, lie buried in those figures? Twenty-nine per cent have at least seen the inside of a high school, but only 14 per cent have been graduated. Just 10 per cent have been to college, but fewer than half of these have hung on for four years and presumably been graduated.

A calculation of the median number of school years completed for the whole country's adults is 8.4, with the city median at 8.7 years, and the rural farm at 7.7. Of city youngsters, 5.7 per cent spent four years at college, but only 1.3 per cent of farm youngsters got as far as that.

The youngsters *under* twenty-five are going to show a better record than those over that age. For one thing, the latter class includes a great many immigrants who came over before the last war, while the former includes very few. We have had practically no immigration in the last eighteen years. A test check of the Census in 1940 shows 95 per cent of all children between seven and fifteen years of age at school, and 56 per cent at ages fifteen to nineteen. We are doing better, but to meet the high-school-for-all standard a great deal more needs to be done.

The gap to be filled in our system of public education is so enormous that it might throw the unwary reader off balance. To regain perspective we must remember that except for some countries in Western Europe, like Sweden, no nation has ever given the mass of its population so much schooling as the United States gives. When we lift our sight to high school for all, it is, in the perspective of history, a very lofty sight. But in the power age I doubt if it is too lofty.

Little Red Schoolhouses

Despite the magnificence of many of our new school buildings, the educational plant still leaves much to be desired. Data prepared by the U.S. Office of Education in 1938 show that of 229,000 public-school buildings in the country, no less than 121,000—more than half—were one-room affairs. In these little red schoolhouses, a single teacher may be instructing pupils in as many as twelve grades. The majority of such teachers, in a ten-state study, were instructing eight grades of pupils. Over 368,000 students if they continued in school would spend their entire elementary school life with one teacher, who would instruct them in every subject in the curriculum. Comparing this with what children receive in the way of instruction and equipment in a modern city school, the most sentimental admirer of the little red schoolhouse must cease to sigh about its virtues. The best answer to the problems of the one-room school, with its encyclopedic teacher, is the rural consolidated school, served by bus. Many of these have been built, but many more are needed.

The fact that the school population is now declining has

been seized on in some quarters to prove that we shall need fewer teachers. This is true only in part. We need more teachers for kindergartens and more teachers for high schools, while the number of teachers required in grade schools depends not only on the number of pupils but on the most efficient teaching load. The number of children per teacher is too high in many areas. Furthermore, if all children attend grade school through the last grade, as they should, a large force of additional teachers will be needed.

Of all persons over twenty-five years of age in the District of Columbia, only 11 per cent have been graduated from any college. In Arkansas the figure is 2 per cent. In these Budget estimates I have not raised the question of college education at all. I have been looking only at the problem of giving a high-school education to every normal child. There are many students in college today who are getting nothing out of it. There are hundreds of thousands of talented boys and girls who have not had the opportunity to go to college. If these talents are wasted in unemployment or dead-end occupations, the nation loses a great community asset. Sooner or later a way should be found to open college doors for those youngsters who ought to go, and to remove from college those youngsters who may have more aptitude for boiler-making and open-field running than for the higher learning.

The Budget Program

Education is accepted as the universal right of every American child. The tasks outlined for us here are to expand educational opportunities in the lower and upper age groups, to abolish child labor and get the youngsters back into school, to level up opportunities between city and country, between one state and another, to eliminate illiteracy, to build more modern schoolhouses, to train a great new army of teachers.

This army may vary from 400,000 to twice that number, or more, depending on the standards set. Like the other items in the Budget, this one is elastic. A national minimum standard does not by any means need to be a bare subsistence standard. Each time it is raised, however, a controversy ensues. Remember the bitter denunciations of New York City schools, a few years ago, for teaching music, art, athletics.

Perhaps 500,000 additional teachers is as good a mark as any to shoot at. The standard is a single-minded one: improve education enough to prepare citizens to do average power-age jobs, and enough to give them reasonable protection against demagogues like Huey Long.

Of the curriculum and the quality of education we shall say nothing. That is another story. We should be arguing here all night.

9
THE PLANT

IN 1929, according to the National Survey, the United States had farms and factories capable of producing an adequate supply of consumers' goods for every family in the country. The Budget could have been met in that year, had it been a national objective. It was not our objective. The operators of the farm-and-factory plant were not concerned, and not supposed to be concerned, with seeing to it that all Americans got enough to eat. They were chiefly concerned with their personal objectives of getting enough to eat, wear and spend for themselves.

This was the correct, orthodox way to do things in 1929. The depression had not come with its threat of mass hunger. The war had not come with its threat to national survival. Mr. Hoover, however, cast a wistful eye toward the Budget from time to time, and so did a number of farsighted engineers and businessmen. They talked about two cars, not in *some* garages, but in *every* garage, and about the end of poverty. They talked about the "new era" which mass production seemed to be bringing. Heigh-ho, it did not come, but it is interesting to remember that they talked about it. After the war the new era may really come.

During the early years of the depression, the national plant suffered through lack of maintenance and repair. After 1935, according to the figures of Dr. Alvin Hansen, the depletion was largely made good as the national income climbed from 40 to 70 billions.[1] Meanwhile all studies showed a striking increase in output per man hour during the depression. Industrial managers had to keep costs down, and labor-saving devices were the way to do it.

If the National Survey or some other responsible organization had made a parallel study based on the farm-and-factory plant in 1940, it is safe to say that the Budget would have been no harder to meet than in 1929. Quite possibly it would have been easier. New inventions, new agricultural machinery and methods, new photoelectric cell devices, new processes, had been steadily developed, while population gained only 7 per cent during the decade.

The Streamlined Postwar Plant

What is the war going to do to the country's productive plant? Unless it is such a long war that resources and plant are drained away to an extent not now anticipated, the war promises to step up our productive capacity to unprecedented heights. Already on the horizon are tremendous increases in the generation of electric power, in machine tools, in the production of light metals, synthetic rubber, plastics, plywood, steel, aircraft, chemicals, ships. Listen to C. E. Wilson, president of the General Electric Company:[2]

> Every industry doing war work should be readying itself for the peacetime transformation. While working on the complicated weap-

1. *TNEC Hearings,* Part 9, Exhibit 543.
2. Article in the *New Leader,* May 1942.

ons of modern warfare, we are daily making new discoveries in electronics, metallurgy, chemistry, synthetics, plastics, aeronautics, and a dozen other fields. All these things help to build a reservoir for tomorrow. . . . The new discoveries in science are being matched by new advances in engineering and the techniques of production. The making of gun barrels can teach us something about the making of electric motors. The shortage of certain strategic materials has opened the road to the new plastics industry that will never be closed again. Housing for armed forces and defense workers improves the technique of building cheaper homes for all of us.

Thurman Arnold is just as hopeful.[3] The last war brought us modern mass production and a whole new chemical industry, as by-products. This war is going to launch us into an age of light metals. "Patent bottlenecks," says Mr. Arnold, "are going to be broken. Knowledge and skill are going to be disseminated. . . . Before the war there was only one magnesium and one aluminum producer in the United States. Today, a court decree has broken the international cartel that restricted magnesium production to a few thousand tons a year to prevent it from competing with aluminum. . . . After the war there will be as many as ten magnesium producers and four aluminum producers." Magnesium and aluminum, now rolling forth in giant quantities for bombers and munitions, will roll into automobiles, trucks, busses, railroad trains, farm machinery, prefabricated houses, after the war. "Welding and the use of light metals offer undreamed-of possibilities in home construction." Not to be outdone, the makers of electric-furnace and alloy steels have increased plant capacity 85 per cent since the war started. Faced with this competition, copper and brass, says Mr. Arnold, will have to come way down in price, plumbing fixtures will be

3. *The Saturday Evening Post,* May 30, 1942.

cheap, and a bathroom will no longer be in the Cadillac class.[4]

Out in Detroit the automotive industry is working at a rate far above normal production—when the only output was motorcars and trucks. One company is said to have cut the time for making a British antiaircraft gun by four months, and evolved a way of broaching the barrel that reduces the time for this operation from three and a half hours to fifteen minutes. Another company has invented equipment for making machine guns that beats regular arsenal machinery by twenty to thirty times. Another has brought the cost of automatic cannon from $1,800 to $600. A new flame-cutting process turns out twelve tank-engine sprockets in six minutes, where it used to take eight hours for a single sprocket![5] The full story of wartime industrial efficiency is a military secret. When someday it is told, it will make you proud to be an American.

The word is abroad that the automobile companies are going to scrap their dies for 1942 cars, and begin over again from scratch when the war ends. *Time* has presented a drawing of the car we may get when we can buy cars again. The artist shows something almost too good to be true—not a wallowing, superpowered, chromium-plated monster, but a lean, clean car at $300 in 1942 prices. It will be truly streamlined, in contrast with the present phony streamlining. Like a gunner in a flying fortress we shall look out through a transparent plastic top. . . . Bodies of plastic panels, tougher than steel. . . . Smaller wheels than at present, with long-wearing synthetic tires. . . . Better weight-to-horsepower ratio, 100-octane gasoline instead of the present

4. A good prewar bathroom cost about $1,000.

5. *Time,* June 15, 1942.

74 in the tank, and 50 miles or more to the gallon. . . . Engine in the rear, with hood as storage space for tires, battery, air conditioner. . . . Undercarriage closed in and streamlined. . . . Doors and windows operated by push button. . . . Top speed, 60 miles per hour—fast enough for all but fools! In short, real transportation.

Fifty Per Cent More Energy

When all is said and done, energy governs the material aspects of any civilization. Low-energy cultures depend on the conversion of energy from food to human and animal muscle. Higher-energy cultures depend on the conversion of energy from coal to steam. The power age depends on the conversion of energy from coal, oil and falling water to electric current, measured in kilowatt-hours. If living standards depend broadly on kilowatt-hours, we are going to take a dizzy ride aloft in the next few years. A report by the Brookings Institution, released in July 1942, estimates our ascending power requirements as follows:

1941	production	212 billion kilowatt-hours
1942	estimated requirements	249 " " "
1943	" "	285 " " "
1944	" "	305 " " "
1945	" "	326 " " "

If we build generators to meet the requirements, the increase in capacity by the end of 1945 will be just about 50 per cent—assuming that full capacity was used in 1941. Demand can be temporarily balanced with capacity by daylight saving, dimming advertising signs, neon lights, street lights, and by rationing consumers. But as the war demand really begins to mount, nothing but new steam plants and hydroelectric dams can meet it.

The General Electric Company, alone, according to its President, Mr. C. E. Wilson, has orders on hand for 19 million horsepower of generating equipment. If this should all go into steam and hydroelectric plants, it would increase U.S. capacity by no less than 34 per cent.[6] Just one company's contribution!

We may end the war with an energy capacity half again as great as when we entered it. This means that if we turn our hand to making goods for the Budget, the flow cannot fail to be ample, including many mass comforts as well as the basic wants.

Fifteen Billions of Investment

In 1938, the plant of the automobile industry was valued at approximately one billion dollars. With this as a bench mark, let us see what has been appropriated for new industrial plants since the defense program got under way in 1940. The figures are only to the fall of 1941. Since Pearl Harbor few figures have been released.

Government appropriations for new plants and equipment	$6.2 billions
Private defense plant expansion program	1.0 "
Total to September 1, 1941	$7.2 billions

That is seven times as great as the whole automobile industry. It is more than one third as great as the entire expenditure for manufacturing plant in the whole decade of

6. *Time,* June 8, 1942. (Some of the equipment is undoubtedly destined for the Navy, and some is probably going abroad.)

the 1920's. Here are the industries chiefly affected:

Aircraft	$848,000,000
Ammunition	806,000,000
Chemical	627,000,000
Shipbuilding	585,000,000
Iron and steel	498,000,000
Nonferrous metals, aluminum, magnesium, etc.	325,000,000
Guns and artillery	285,000,000
Machine tools	240,000,000

Other large appropriations went to build new factories for electrical equipment, tanks, instruments of precision. Remember that this is all *capital construction*—not one penny for the actual production of anything. The bombers, tanks and destroyers are covered by separate appropriations.

By February 1, 1942, total government contracts let for war plants had increased almost another billion to $7,100,000,000. A map of the United States showing these new plants indicates a policy of decentralization.[7] New England, New York, Pennsylvania, get relatively less. The Great Lakes region holds its own, but the South, the Tennessee Valley, Texas, the Northwest, the West Coast, and the Rocky Mountain region get relatively more new factories.

In May 1942, Jesse Jones asked Congress for $5 billion more for war plants. He got it. On July 1, 1942, the U.S. Information Service said that "government commitments for war-plant expansion during the period from June 1940, to April 1942, were made to 1,644 projects and totalled $12,131,000,000." Private company commitments during the same period were made to 7,832 projects to a total of $2,974,-

7. *Time,* June 1, 1942.

000,000. Since January 1942, the breakdown of these totals, says the Information Service, has been a military secret.

Thus no less than $15 billions, or fifteen times the plant investment of the whole automobile industry, has been so far allocated for new plants. A big chunk of it has recently gone into synthetic rubber factories, with a production goal of more than 1,000,000 tons a year. . . . Don't ask me to specify whether the rubber will be made from alcohol, petroleum or soapsuds. . . . Some plants which have been ordered are not being developed at the moment, for lack of steel and other raw materials. Whether the whole $15 billion will turn into concrete and steel I do not know. But we know that a large fraction of it already has done so, and the war seems to be a long way from being won as I write. The final effect on the industrial plant of America staggers the imagination. It also promises to delight the eye, for the new factories are being constructed on the odd and unusual assumption that human beings, not just "hands," are to work in them.

The capacity of the machine-tool industry stands in somewhat the same relation to the standard of living as does power. Here is where the lathes, drills, milling machines, shapers, broaching machines, grinders, are made without which neither guns nor planes, motorcars nor refrigerators, can in turn be produced. These are the machines which make the machines of the power age. In 1940, 100,000 units were produced by the machine-tool industry, where a normal year called for 25,000. In 1941, 200,000 units were produced; in 1942 it looks like 300,000. The entire stock of machine tools on hand in 1939 was estimated by OPM at 330,000. So before this war is over we are going to have two or three times as many machines to make machines as we had when it began. Machine tools can be adjusted to make an oil heater, a washing machine, a prefabricated house, as well as a tank or a field gun. Some tools, to be sure, are especially designed for one job, but many are "general-purpose" machines. A screw machine can make screws for an antitank gun or for a farm tractor. This is not to deny, however, that the task of reconversion to peacetime production will be a huge one.

More Self-Sufficiency

While the war will, of course, deplete some natural resources to an unpredictable extent, the decline of imports from the Old World has greatly stimulated new sources in this hemisphere. Besides synthetic rubber, we are developing the following. It is only a partial list.

Aluminum from local clays.
Manganese from low-grade U.S. ores by new process.
New tungsten deposits in U.S. expected to triple 1939 output.
New magnesium sources discovered and worked.
New chromium deposits in Oregon and Montana.
New vanadium deposits in Ontario.
New nickel deposits in Cuba.
China clays in Carolina.
Rubber and high-octane gasoline produced simultaneously.
Synthetic quinine—called Atabrine.
Substitutes for tin cans, especially lacquers on black plate.
Plastics from soybeans and corn.
Vinyl esters (a plastic family) for shoes, aprons, smocks, capes, umbrellas, heel pads.
Textiles, from blankets to handkerchiefs, made of wood pulp.
Other textiles—wool, crepe and linen substitutes—from casein.
Textiles from spun glass.
Many new uses for plywood, some of them revolutionary.
The vast project of the United Fruit Company to grow crops for hemp, quinine, rubber, palm oil, in Central America.

After the war we may have more airplane factories than we shall know what to do with—even counting on a foolproof job for civilians to keep in the backyard—and metal furniture, prefabricated housing panels, radiant heat units, to be made in the ex-bomber plants. The whole nation will be studded with magnificent new airfields. There is a chance, however, that a substantial fraction of the airplane industry will be kept very busy indeed. Here is a lyrical description from a news column:

> Out of the tragic destruction of war, out of the tons of steel sent daily to the ocean's bottom, out of the cities wrecked and lives lost, will come a great forward thrust for aviation—a network of airlines spanning the world like a spiderweb. For today the Air Forces Air Ferrying Command is conducting operations on a larger scale than all the civilian airlines of the U.S. put together. And in a few months, when present plans are completed, its operations will be *ten times larger than all the civil airlines of the world before the war began!* Says Brigadier General Harold L. George, Chief of the Ferrying Command: "We are transport agent for the world. We are picking up planes in California and putting them down a few days later in Egypt, Persia, India, Australia, Alaska, Russia, Great Britain—any place you want to name. Our operations offices are scattered from here to the ends of the earth. No airline was ever conceived on such a scale. And after the war—well! that's something to think about."[8]

It is one of many things to think about. More airlines, more electric power, more machine tools, more aluminum and magnesium plants, iron and steel mills, metal refineries, shipyards, synthetic and plastic works, raw-material deposits, and all manner of new industrial techniques—these are some of the by-products the war is going to lay upon our doorstep. Some factories may be bombed, some, like powder plants, may be boarded up after the war is over. The net effect of the

8. Drew Pearson and Robert S. Allen, May 23, 1942.

war on American productive capacity, however, cannot fail to be staggering.

The Green Light

The editors of *Business Week*[9] have boldly laid before us a revolutionary question concerning our industrial plant. It is difficult to overestimate the importance of the problem they raise:

> The potentialities of mass production have amazed even the experts in mass production. By comparison, this country has never had real mass production before. The production men have always been limited by the market. Now, for the first time, we have thrown in the switch and left it in. . . . American industry is learning how it can run with the wraps off. It is learning what it can do when its best production brains are allowed to go wide-open, when the only limits on the production facilities it can use are the limits on the time and materials needed to fabricate those facilities. . . .
>
> What it all comes down to is that American industry is learning how it could and would operate the production machine in an economy of abundance—and, so far as sheer production technique is concerned, it makes little difference that the market is an artificial one . . . and the abundance is death. Those who talk of victory and in the same breath of American industry unable, after victory, to apply the lessons of all-out production to a peacetime market, and a free price system under the rules of competitive enterprise, are simply overlooking a bet to which the record should now be tipping them off.

Ever since 1925, when I wrote a book called *The Tragedy of Waste,* I have been arguing that if the technical men were given permission to operate their machines on an all-out basis, we should be literally deluged with goods. The war has brought this argument to the acid test. It appears to be sound. We never had real mass production before, says

9. Issue of May 30, 1942.

Business Week. Are we going to abandon it when the war is over? We never had it before because there has never before been a market broad enough to absorb the output. Why this has been so need not concern us here. Now the market is available. It is the Army, Navy, Air Force, Maritime Commission, thundering for output, more output and more output. As it thunders, industry, hesitatingly[10] at first, then faster and faster, roars into a rate of production unprecedented and unknown!

The lesson is there for all to read. If the production men are not thwarted by the exigencies of buying cheap and selling dear, if the only goal of the production men is production, they can make the plant jump over the moon. Will they have to crawl back into their shells after they have so magnificently demonstrated their ability? Will large sections of the plant be frozen lifeless because the death business is ended, and people now are demanding goods for life?

This is going to be the greatest challenge that American businessmen have ever faced. It will be up to them to prove to their fellow countrymen that full production and free enterprise can work in harness. If, after this wartime lesson, they try to bottle up the production experts, lead industry back to the crippled, part-time, monopoly-choked operation of the 1930's, it is probable that both their fellow countrymen and the production experts will look somewhere else for industrial leadership. If a man getting $50 a week is suddenly cut to $25, for no good reason, he is likely to resent it.

It is very encouraging to have *Business Week* state the

10. Before Pearl Harbor, many businessmen were afraid to expand their plants much because of "excess capacity" after the war. Now they have no choice.

problem thus early in the game. Every businessman in the country should start thinking about it now. He should be asking himself how he can co-operate with other businessmen to maintain a high rate of production—with less overtime to be sure—on a high-volume, low-price basis, when the war ends. He should be planning *now*—as the General Electric Company and various other companies are planning—for new and improved products to manufacture when there are no longer guns to manufacture. He should be thinking about taking his share of responsibility for full employment.

The trouble with prewar business was its lack of responsibility for making the economic system work. True, the theory was that it would work without anybody taking responsibility. The theory was exploded in 1929. The war is showing us what the economic system can do in the way of production when everybody takes responsibility—businessmen, workingmen, government men, professional men, housewives, Boy Scouts, everybody. The future of American business probably turns on holding such an attitude. How far this may conflict with earlier theories, and with concepts of free enterprise, is a question which businessmen must squarely face.

10
PUBLIC WORKS

NOBODY WHO USES his eyes has failed to see that when war spending started, unemployment began to decline. The connection was too obvious to be missed. Most economists now agree that any depression involving large numbers of unemployed men can be broken if somebody spends enough to put citizens to work. Spending for lethal weapons will do it, spending for bailing out the Great Lakes will do it, spending for old-age pensions will do it—provided the senior citizens promptly spend their allowances; spending to build cathedrals will do it. The only qualification is that *enough be spent* to put virtually everybody to work. This the New Deal never did; this the war has done.

A natural conclusion from this object lesson is that any threatened postwar collapse can be averted by government outlays. The most obvious outlay is public works—instead of powder plants, for instance, a Grand Coulee dam. Furthermore, public works between wars is a simpler way to maintain full employment than regulating everybody's business by government fiat, or by rationing everybody. In the early 1920's, Mr. Hoover, as Secretary of Commerce, appointed a commission to work on details for such a balance wheel. The idea is not new.

Under the public-works theory, private businessmen go ahead and sell all they can. If they cannot put all the idle to work, the government steps in and builds highways, dams or schoolhouses until the unemployed are absorbed. This keeps wages up, sales up, jobs up, and debts up. The first three results are fine and the last is not so fine, but there it is. Those who object must offer a practicable alternative.

The American Youth Commission, under the chairmanship of Owen D. Young, has stated the basic assumptions in a report which can be summarized as follows:[1]

1. The successful prosecution of the war is the most important problem confronting the American people today.
2. When the war ends, full employment will be the most urgent national objective.
3. Changes in the American economic system, which have been going on for fifty years and are now much accelerated, will not present insuperable barriers to full employment, but will necessitate some fundamental economic readjustments.
4. For some years after the war, the attempt to achieve full employment through the expansion of private enterprise will be only partially successful. It will be necessary to carry on substantial programs of public works to provide jobs for everybody.

Broadly interpreted, public works include not only physical things that are built, but also services rendered in the public interest and administered by the government. We ordinarily define public works in terms of something you can kick with your foot, like a concrete bridge; but so far as employment is concerned, it can just as well refer to a program for adult education, a federal arts project, food allow-

1. *Youth and the Future,* General Report of the Commission, 1942.

ances for expectant mothers, dental clinics, old-age pensions, research projects, planting trees.

The National Resources Planning Board and the Federal Works Agency in Washington have been working on a great "shelf" of public works to fill the gap in postwar employment. The projects include federal, state and local outlays. New York City has plans for more than $600 million worth of public works saved up for the future, including hospitals, harbor improvements, schoolhouses, fire stations, libraries, museums, parks, viaducts, bridges, sewers, courthouses. New York State has a reservoir of $60 million for highways and parks, $40 million for grade-crossing elimination, $220 million for housing.[2]

We must remember that public works can cut in two directions. They provide employment when employment is otherwise unobtainable, but many of them also are *necessary for community survival,* quite apart from the question of employment. Their maintenance may be an essential industry. Suppose private business in a big boom tried to hire all the employees of the New York City water department. Should they go and leave eight million people without water?

The great divisions of physical public works are housing, remaking our cities, watershed development and conservation, and modernizing the national transportation system. Let us consider them briefly.[3]

Government Housing

This subject has been discussed earlier at some length.

2. Reported in *The New York Times,* May 11, 1942.

3. *Guides for Post-War Planning,* Pamphlet No. 8, National Planning Association, November 1941; *Better Cities,* by Charles S. Ascher, National Resources Planning Board, April 1942.

Mr. C. F. Palmer, at the Fortune Round Table, called for 600,000 housing units a year to be subsidized by the government, 1,000,000 units to be financed by private industry. Housing will be the greatest single outlet for re-employment after the war. It also fits solidly in the agenda of the Budget.

Urban Redevelopment

If this division of public works should really get going, it could become even larger than the housing program. It calls for a gradual rebuilding of our cities, practically from the ground up, to meet the requirements of the power age. Some cities, like Boston, were built in the handicraft age. Others, like Chicago, were built in the railway-coal age. No American city has yet been built for the age of electric power, motor traffic, aircraft and light metals. The only exceptions are a handful of towns like Radburn near New York, and Greenbelt near Washington, which have been deliberately constructed for living in the power age.

To live in our great cities today requires courage, fortitude and iron nerves. Personally, I admit that I am not strong enough to do more than visit them occasionally, and return to my Connecticut farm suffering from nervous indigestion. The cities are dark, dirty, noisy, overcrowded, jammed with traffic, replete with slums, blighted areas and dreary reaches of a monumental ugliness. Even their bright spots cannot redeem them. The Chicago lake front makes back-of-the-yards in Chicago still more terrible by contrast. Megalopolis has approached its limit, both physically and financially. Hardly a skyscraper has been built since 1932. Real-estate values in most cities have been falling for years, and tax receipts with them. Under any kind of a postwar world, a major financial operation will be absolutely necessary.

Cities should be replanned and rebuilt, says Mr. Ascher, not by the block but by the square mile. Neighborhoods should be designed for living, so that citizens may know their neighbors and feel that they belong to a functioning community again. The plan should deal with the whole urban area and not be limited by artificial boundaries. Thus New York involves not only the legal city, but large sections of Westchester County, New Jersey and Connecticut. The plan should aim to make the resources of the city more freely available to the surrounding country dwellers, and the resources of the country more available to city dwellers. The legal and financial procedure for acquiring land should be simplified and speeded up. Federal aid will undoubtedly be needed in financing and planning. Slums should be cleared and blighted areas levelled for parks. Playgrounds, schools, hospitals, harbor and river improvements, parking facilities should be redesigned on a grand scale.

Take the single item of water pollution. Only a quarter of all American city sewage is now properly treated. The wastes of 35 million people are dumped, untreated, into city rivers and harbors. If it happens to be a river, the "law of dumping down" is followed, whereby the town next below is presented with typhoid germs from the town above. The PWA in recent years has built 1,500 sewer systems, and 2,400 urban water systems. Such work obviously should go on until every city in the country is protected.

Eliel Saarinen, the architect who designed the famous railway station at Helsingfors, is working in his laboratory near Detroit on fundamental methods for redesigning modern cities. He calls his method *organic decentralization.* The well-planned city, he says, must be conceived not only on maps, but in three dimensions as well. The towering structures, tree-lined boulevards, stretches of green belt, public squares, and modest homes and shops must all fit into place as integral parts of a beautiful, closely woven pattern. He is developing such a pattern for Detroit, Cleveland and Chicago. In Flint and Saginaw, Michigan, his plans are actually being tried out.[4]

Multiple-Purpose Dams, Watershed Control, Conservation

The classic example for this variety of public works is the TVA. Here a great river is controlled from source to mouth by a handful of technicians pulling switches in powerhouses. They store water here, let it out there, raise or lower the channel depth, increase or diminish the hydroelectric head. No such comprehensive technical control has ever before been applied to any river in the world. But similar programs are being worked out for the Columbia and for the rivers of the Central Valley of California. Every major watershed in the nation would benefit by similar treatment. Here are some of the purposes served:

The generation of cheap power for consumers and industry. Four million farmhouses are still without current, together with rural schools, churches, stores, mills.

Flood control, by means of reservoirs to hold back the floodwaters, headwater planting to slow runoff, and levees in the lower reaches.

Erosion control, with forests on the steep slopes, grass on the less steep slopes, croplands plowed on the contours below.

Navigation. The importance of our inland waterways is now being dramatically underlined by sinkings of coastwise ships and the resulting oil shortage. The TVA is completing a 600-mile channel

4. See article in *Time,* July 7, 1942.

from the Ohio to Knoxville, which will be useful in peace as well as war.

Irrigation. Grand Coulee Dam will irrigate an area of rich farm land as large as Delaware.

Control of the underground water table. In some watersheds the level of underground water has dropped fifty feet, which means that citizens have to dig their wells deeper and deeper to get less and less water. Over-all watershed control can hold rain on the land, check runoff and replenish the underground supply. This is a particularly important factor in the Central Valley of California, where the great Shasta Dam is being built.

Recreation—swimming, fishing, boating, summer cottages, camping, hiking. The Tennessee River is now a linked series of huge lakes, each of which is rapidly turning into a vital recreation center.

Closely allied with watershed control is the whole problem of conservation. The National Resources Planning Board has estimated that a million workers, representing almost every occupation, could be kept busy at the task of merely holding our forests, grasslands, waters, wild life—our basic wealth—at par.

Take forestry alone. When the Pilgrims landed there were more than 460 million acres of magnificent forest land. Only 100 million acres of virgin stand remain, mostly in the Northwest. We are cutting, burning and destroying trees much faster than nature is growing them. To hold this resource at par, says the United States Forest Service, growth should be doubled.[5] Here are the types of work such a program entails:

Replanting cutover lands.
Fire control.
Insect control.

5. *New Forest Frontiers,* U.S. Forest Service, Miscellaneous Publication 414, April 1941.

Thinning and cutting public forests.

Completing the forest survey of the United States—now only half-done.

Planning "permanent-yield" communities where forests can be cut forever.

More forest research.

Restoring range productivity (grazing land within forests).

Restoring wild life and game.

Planning public campgrounds and low-cost vacation areas, which will make our forests really available to the people.

Bringing Transportation Up to Date

Many of our roads were built for stagecoaches. Some of our canals were built before the railroads. Most of our railroads were built before the motorcar, the truck and the airplane. The net result is pretty much of a scramble, with efficiency blocked by obsolete facilities and equipment, by duplications, competing terminals, parking jams, traffic jams, high costs generally. America with its continental distances depends on transport more than any other nation, except possibly Russia. The time has come to bring the system up to date, to throw the whole organism into the mold of the power age.

This promises to be a whale of a job. It means using waterways for slow, heavy freight and giving up the operation of inefficient canals and rivers just because they happen to lie in some congressman's district. It means using railroads for long hauls, trucks for short hauls, and scrapping many short-haul feeder lines which the railroads now maintain at excessive cost. These are the lines where the rails are rusty and grass grows high between the ties. Sky trucks must also be allowed for after the war, with airfields to land them on.

It means a lot more super highways, and new light metal cars and trucks to move over them. It means unscrambling duplicate terminal facilities in the cities, and co-ordinating harbors, docks, freight yards, airports and trucking terminals. It means eliminating dangerous grade crossings, building new bridges, ramps, under- and overpasses. It means a rate structure which will encourage both passengers and freight to use that form of transport where the least energy is expended and the cost is lowest.

I once made a study in man-hour costs covering various types of transportation for the National Resources Planning Board.[6] The operating cost to move a thousand tons of freight one mile varies as follows:

Man pushing a wheelbarrow	20,000 man hours
Five-ton truck	50.0 " "
Class I railroads, freight department	5.8 " "
Inland waterways	4.7 " "
Oil pipe lines	2.0 " "

On the basis of some such physical costs as these, the integrated transport system should be worked out. Obviously the above figures need refining, especially in respect to including plant costs, before they can be used. They just indicate an approach to the engineer's ideal of getting the most for the least.

To these four main classes of public works, a fifth might be added, under the heading of "public services." In the first book in this series, *The Road We Are Traveling,* I described the powerful trend in the United States toward more

6. Report of December 1, 1934. The reason the truck beats the railroad in spite of its higher cost on a cross-country run, is that it can go from factory door to customer's door on a short run.

and more employment in the so-called "service trades," at the cost of agricultural and manufacturing employment. The Census shows more than half of our gainfully employed in the service class, as clerks, doctors, nurses, teachers, roadside attendants, accountants, government employees, salesmen, insurance agents, and so on. C. Hartley Grattan, among others, has gone so far as to lay down a law in this connection. As technology enables us to produce a ton of potatoes or a ton of steel with less and less cost measured in man hours, jobs in agriculture and manufacturing are bound to decline in the long run. Where are new jobs to be found? In the service trades. And this is precisely where they have been found in recent years. The machine takes over, releasing men for lighter tasks. This is the progression:

1. Agricultural regions tend to have low living standards. Look at China, India, the cotton belt in the United States.

2. Manufacturing regions have higher living standards always. Look at Victorian England.

3. When an economy has a large proportion of its workers in the service trades, its living standards tend to rise still higher. Look at the United States in the last half century.

In any discussion of public works or public employment down the years, it is important to recognize this one, two, three progression, fostered by the pressure of technology and invention. For some time to come there will be opportunities for employment in making and moving things—foodstuffs, housing, manufactured goods, hospitals, dams and highways. But for the long view, both private and public employment will move increasingly toward the services. Public "services" may even become more important on the employment front than public "works," defined as physical construction. These services we already have, and they are cardinal in certain sectors of the Budget, but they can be expected to expand enormously. They include medical workers of all kinds; educational workers of all kinds; scientists, psychologists, anthropologists and technicians; administrative staffs; recreational directors; research personnel; artists, writers, actors, musicians.

Public Works and the Budget

None of the physical projects listed above is novel in kind. We have heard a great deal about all of them since 1933, and have made some exciting beginnings. It is the scale of the work that is new, a scale in proportion to the size of the nation. The work required to develop the United States as intensively as England, for instance, has been developed, staggers the imagination. We have a magnificent country but it is still full of raw, unfinished areas.

Of the four great outlets for public works, government-sponsored houses are in the budget of shelter. Urban redevelopment projects having to do with hospitals, sanitation, stream pollution, are in the budget of health. Projects having to do with school building are in the budget of education. Watershed improvement, conservation and the integration of transportation affect the Big Five at many points.

If we shift our frame of reference a little, we can cease to think of these items as "public works" at all, but rather as integral parts of the Budget. In the interest of community welfare it is far more important that they be done than that man power be devoted to useless luxuries, gadgets and superfluities—say annual models for motorcars, patent nostrums, the more exotic branches of the cosmetic trade.

There remains an element in many public-works programs which is not of immediate utility, but which can serve both civilization and employment. Take, for instance, redesigning and rebuilding our cities. The project is a challenge to the enduring civilization we hope to make in America. It calls for our boldest and most inspired engineering, architectural and administrative ability. The world's fairs at New York, Chicago, San Francisco, gave a hint of the magnificence of the vision. This is no make-work proposal, but something to last down the ages as the pyramids of the Mayas, the temples of the Greeks, the cathedrals of Europe, have lasted.

When the war ends, the people of Europe too must have a Budget. The first task will be to establish order. The second task will be to feed the hungry and guard against epidemics. The third task will be a vast reconstruction program to get the transport and energy systems flowing again, and houses, factories, hospitals, churches, docks, warehouses, rebuilt. We can and should help Europe with food, supplies, medicines and technical aid for the huge public-works program.

It is interesting to watch the career of that miracle man of the west, Henry J. Kaiser. Here is a private businessman who has won his reputation, his fortune, and the gratitude of the whole nation, almost solely in the field of public works. His first great achievement was Boulder Dam. Then came Grand Coulee, Shasta, and the Golden Gate bridge. Now he is making ships to government order at a speed never matched before, and he wants to build sky trucks with which to win the war.

I think there is some kind of a moral here for those who insist that public business is evil and private business is good —or vice versa. Mr. Kaiser shows us how a businessman can co-operate with the public interest to the greater glory of both. If we had another score like him they could rebuild the whole country in towering splendor over the next decade or two!

11
TAKING INVENTORY

THIS STUDY makes no pretense of being the final word on national minimum standards. It documents a trend, an answer to the world-wide demand for economic security. The figures given have not been checked by an authoritative body consecrated to the Budget of national minimum standards. No authoritative body, private or governmental, is so consecrated yet.[1] The National Resources Planning Board has probably given the subject more attention than any other agency. All I have tried to do is to gather a sample of such figures as are available from dependable sources, make certain calculations from the figures, and use the result to illustrate a thesis. Let us recapitulate the thesis.

The war can be considered as one aspect of a gigantic social revolution. We are in the midst of one of the great transition periods of history, where economic, political and social institutions are changing at an abnormal rate. In the first book of this series, *The Road We Are Traveling,* I tried to show the pattern of these changes over the past quarter

1. The Twentieth Century Fund has in preparation a detailed study of the Budget, involving a large research staff.

century. As the change accelerates, a mounting demand is heard from the mass of the people everywhere for jobs, security, hope. They rally to the support of leaders who promise them these things. A postwar settlement, external or internal, which does not give expression to this mass demand will settle nothing. The fire will presently burn through. The Atlantic Charter recognized this, but its promises were vague. We have been trying, in this book, to sharpen the concept of "freedom from want," to give it physical body as applied to America.

Economic rights must be squarely based on economic duties and sacrifices. One makes no sense without the other. As in the edict of Captain John Smith of Virginia, those who eat must work. No strong community with a high factor of survival can be built on the shaky foundations of chronic unemployment, handouts and doles. How to tie these duties and rights together and enlarge our democratic framework to include them may be our major postwar political problem.

The economic rights include what we have called the Big Five: food, shelter, clothing, health services, education for the last child in the community. There is no physical reason why many mass comforts, such as motorcars, may not be added to the essentials.

The concrete details of such standards depend not only on the trained man power available, but on natural resources, inanimate energy, the productive plant, and the public plant, reflected in such assets as hospitals, school buildings and conservation projects. Our survey, rough as it is, indicates that all elements are available in America to meet the standards we have suggested for the Budget, and considerably more.

Applying the Budget in 1940

In 1940 we had eight to nine million persons unemployed or on government work-relief projects. We had millions more on part time. We had a reserve of man power on the farms, and in the persons of several million women who did not have much to do at home. This reserve is now being heavily drawn upon for the war effort. In some classes of skills it is entirely exhausted.

Suppose the Budget had been introduced in 1940. Our earlier estimates indicate that to meet its requirements:

No additional man power was needed for food. The crop pattern would have to be shifted somewhat.

To provide adequate shelter, perhaps 2,000,000 workers would be needed for a decade or more, building 1,500,000 units a year. In 1940, 600,000 dwelling units were actually constructed. So the *increase* in the labor force would have been something over 1,000,000.

To provide adequate clothing, 250,000 more workers would be needed on a "bare essentials" basis, perhaps 1,000,000 on a "comfort" basis.

To keep the whole nation healthy would provide jobs for some 300,000 more dentists, doctors, nurses, and perhaps as many more for lay personnel in hospitals and clinics. Say 600,000 at the outside.

To provide education for all children through high school, and to enlarge the scope of adult education, might call for 500,000 more teachers and other workers in the field of education.

Thus somewhere between 3,000,000 and 4,000,000 workers, added to the force of 1940, would have come close to balancing the Budget. And we had better than 8,000,000 to draw from! Obviously this is only the roughest of comparisons, for the unemployed of 1940 did not include enough trained teachers, dentists, nurses, to meet Budget demands. They did include, however, enough construction workers and clothing workers.

Fifteen Million Jobs

What will be the situation in man power when the war ends? We cannot, of course, calculate it with any precision. The changes week by week are too colossal and too rapid. But we can make some rough estimates, based on certain broad assumptions. Let us assume that the armed services and the war industries at the war's end are employing 30,-000,000 citizens, and that 30,000,000 more are working on the production of consumers' goods—including food and clothing for the armed services. The standard of living will be more equitably shared than it was in 1940, owing to price fixing and rationing, but the total output of consumers' goods, especially durable goods and luxuries, will be substantially less than in 1940.

Let us assume that 5,000,000 persons remain in the armed services and war industries when peace comes, and that another 5,000,000 devote themselves to supplying food and equipment to other nations exhausted by war, and a third 5,000,000 are completely demobilized and withdraw from the job front altogether. We still have at least 15,000,000 workers available for bringing standards back to the 1940 level, including the production of luxuries, and for guaranteeing the Budget.

This is obviously far more than enough workers. The real problem will not be to find the man power to meet the Big Five, but to find useful work for all the man power no longer engaged in the war effort. This man power, furthermore, will be trained as no other generation of Americans has ever been trained for productive work.

These estimates are rough and ready. Perhaps our policing job will call for more than 5,000,000 in the armed services and defense industries. Perhaps 5,000,000 women, young men and old men, withdrawn from the work front altogether, is too high. In 1919, the estimate was around 2,000,000 so withdrawn. Perhaps we shall not need as many as 5,000,000 to feed and supply the Old World when hostilities cease; it looks like a pretty generous allowance considering that our total agricultural work force is less than 10,000,000.

But our assumption is that these three classes total 15,000,000 workers or thereabouts. That would leave 15,000,000[2] to be transferred to producing peacetime goods and services for the home population. Adding these to the 30,000,000 already employed in the consumer goods industries when the war ends, we have a force of 45,000,000. This force will grow as more men are demobilized from the war services, and from the task of feeding Europe after Europe begins to feed herself again.

The great demand for goods deferred during the war, especially durable goods, might or might not keep the whole 45,000,000 busy for a short time while the shortages were being replaced and the plant reconverted to peacetime production. What then? Then, with the magnificent new plant, the new energy sources, the new techniques to aid them, the working force would undoubtedly be faced with the prospect of wholesale unemployment—if, indeed, they did not face it from the moment the war ended.

The establishment of the Budget, as already noted, would take care of three to four million workers. But the threat of unemployment may be much larger than that. And here

2. The Commission on Postwar Training and Adjustment of Columbia University released a report in July 1942 estimating that 15,000,000 Americans would have to be transferred to peacetime jobs when the war ends. This is a close check with my estimate.

we come to a decision of critical importance. We can put the unemployed on the dole, or at raking leaves, which would mean that we had won the war and lost the peace. Or we can challenge our citizens with the greatest, most splendid, most uplifting series of public works which any civilization ever dreamed of. I have touched on them earlier—whole cities to be rebuilt and decentralized; mighty watersheds to be tamed, like that of the Tennessee; the forests of America to be put on a perpetual yield basis, the grasslands to be restored, the entire transport system to be integrated; civic centers, libraries, museums, research laboratories, universities, public buildings, to reflect an aspiring culture in a new architecture, and reflect it too in sculpture, painting, music, the theatre.

Room can be found in such projects for all the man power we have available. When technology again gives us a surplus of man power someday—as it surely will—then hours of daily labor can come down, vacation periods grow longer.

"How Bold Our Concept"

The British writer, E. H. Carr, tells us how bold our concept of work ought to be:

> The new faith will approach the unemployment problem not by way of prevention but by way of the *creation* of needs vast enough to make a full call on our resources, and morally imperative enough to command the necessary measure of sacrifice to supply them. All frontal attacks on unemployment have failed, and are bound to fail, because the essence of that problem is not to create work for its own sake—a process economically easy but morally impracticable—but to create work destined to fulfill a purpose felt by the community to be worthy of self-sacrifice.[3]

When Mr. Carr says that all frontal attacks on unemployment have failed, he means that the disease lies deeper than

3. E. H. Carr, *Conditions of Peace,* Macmillan, 1942.

just being without a job. He means that the disease cannot be cured by poking around in the scrap barrel and finding odds and ends of jobs for people. A good deal of the WPA effort was along the scrap-barrel line, and people leaned on their shovels and felt thwarted and foolish. Mr. Carr, like Mr. Peter Drucker (quoted in Chapter 1), means that the disease can be cured only by giving citizens *a sense of belonging to the community again,* of doing something vitally useful. They do not want to be charity cases, they want to be active members of the group.

All these conditions are now met in the war—a national purpose of the utmost challenge to be served through work and sacrifice by every citizen. After we have fulfilled the purpose of saving our civilization from its enemies, then we can move forward to fulfill the purpose of making it enduring, extending its benefits to citizens who have never before enjoyed them.

Using What We Have

The specific methods for putting the Budget into effect lie outside the scope of this book. Many of them are now being worked out in the trial and error of war controls. Many of them were in effect, or had been suggested, before the war began. The major principle involved has been underlined earlier: namely, to use existing customs and existing agencies wherever possible. Do not turn the economy upside down.

When directors of the Surplus Commodities Corporation wanted to feed hungry people in a big way, they did not set up a new government feeding station. They went to the retail food dealers of the country with a suggestion for joint action, and between them they evolved the Food Stamp Plan. This plan used the regular retail store machinery. People who needed food went to the corner grocery with their stamps and bought supplies like anybody else. It made them feel more like citizens not to carry a basket to a government warehouse. It made the grocers and meat dealers feel better to add to their volume of business. The plan saved the government a huge task of administration. Everyone was satisfied, and the prime end of getting good food into the stomachs of those who needed it badly, was successfully accomplished.

We have an enormous private business machine already functioning. It would be the height of folly to tear it up by the roots. Even in the war, while most producers no longer have to think much about pushing their sales, and many important decisions have left their hands, their organizations are still in being and most of them will be so after the war.

We should use them. Employ the profit motive as widely as possible. Encourage businessmen to do all they can, and to take responsibility wherever they can. The critical point is to have in the federal government a conning-tower control charged with the duty of plugging any gaps in the front of full employment.

If private businessmen do not want to undertake mass housing except with government financing, then arrange the financing. If doctors are unable to take care of all sick people on the orthodox fee basis, then make it possible to help doctors take care of all sick people. If private business cannot absorb all the unemployed—and it probably cannot—keep the great public works programs going side-by-side with private business.

The sheer fact of full employment, combined with minimum wages high enough to purchase most essentials, would automatically insure a large part of the Budget standards. Adequate clothing would no longer be even a minor problem under such conditions. For the other four departments, certain supplementary steps would have to be taken.

To insure an adequate diet for everyone entails both a program of education and a controlled crop pattern. Between the AAA and the Lend-Lease bill, we already have most of the crop controls or market supports. The change already made in the American crop pattern is astonishing. In July 1942, the Department of Agriculture announced that while fewer acres were ploughed in 1942 than in 1918, farmers will raise 40 per cent more food—the largest, most diversified, most healthful, most vitamin-rich harvest ever gathered anywhere by any nation. Milk, beef and pork are far above their old peaks. Cotton is far below. Wheat, corn and oats are a little below their old records. Soybeans, flaxseed, peanuts and canning vegetables have zoomed. Production of sweet corn, green peas and tomatoes is at an all-time high. Georgia alone has 30,000 new truck gardens this year. We have 24 per cent more milk cows than in 1917, and average output per cow has climbed from 3,743 to 4,742 pounds per year.

A great program of conservation is also necessary. We have one already, but additions may be needed to make good the depletions of war. By restoring and developing the CCC camp idea, we can enlarge the conservation program and make it permanent. At present we are still fortifying diets through the Food Stamp Plan and the school-lunch plan. Perhaps these agencies should continue after the war as machinery to supplement the food standard. Rationing milk for all children who need it, as in New Zealand, might also be a wise measure.

To meet shelter requirements, a huge program of government-subsidized housing is undoubtedly necessary. As Mr. Palmer told the Fortune Round Table, European governments subsidized 20,000,000 dwelling units in the years before the war. There is nothing very startling in following this procedure. Rural units are also needed in large numbers, as our little visit to Uncle Henry made clear. The FSA building programs offer good models to follow here. War housing is producing other exciting models.

To meet health requirements, the Wagner bill or its equivalent should be passed by Congress.[4] As in the case of diet, a big program of health education is essential. More talented young people should go into training to become dentists, technicians, nurses, doctors and psychiatrists. Public works in the form of hospitals, clinics, sanitaria, sewage and pollution-abatement systems are badly needed. Group medicine should be greatly expanded. In short, we should go along the road we are now going, only faster, and more comprehensively. We should go willingly and confidently, not grudgingly and afraid.

Educational standards demand that child labor be eliminated and every normal child be kept in school until he finishes high school. They demand the liquidation of illiteracy among adults. This means the training of many more teach-

4. The preamble of the bill reads as follows: "To provide for the general welfare by enabling the several states to make more adequate provision for public health, prevention and control of disease, maternal and child health services, construction and maintenance of needed hospitals and health centers, disability insurance." 76 Cong., 1 sess. S. 1620, February 27, 1939.

ers and the building of many more schoolhouses. Little red schoolhouses should be sold to artists and suchlike folk. Their function should be transferred to rural consolidated schools where children can get something approaching the educational attention they now receive in cities. Federal aid for schools in low-income areas, especially in the South, is certainly necessary.

If you reread the above administrative suggestions, you will see that most of them are already in operation on a greater or lesser scale. There is nothing revolutionary in this agenda except the will to make it universal; a determination to drive a foundation of economic security under every American. It will give him something firm to stand on for all his life. Equally important, it will serve the fundamental principle of community survival. Finally, it will represent a democracy which runs deeper than any the world has ever seen. In our last chapter we will develop this important point.

12
THE ROAD IS FORWARD

ONE CAN SUMMARIZE the whole question of the Budget as a conflict between the theory of "a lot of bums," and the theory of "give 'em a break." Biologists have given us very definite evidence of late about the capacity of any normal infant to develop into a decent and useful citizen if his early life is not warped by evil surroundings. They will even make an estimate of the number of "superior" individuals who, if equal opportunities are available, can be expected from every thousand normal children. If these biologists are right, Heaven alone knows how many citizens of superior ability we have crucified in our slums and poverty-blighted areas. The "give 'em a break" school of thought stands on both modern biology and Christian ethics.

Two Theories

The theory of "a lot of bums" stands on a fear of the mass of the people, and on a conviction that most men will not work unless threatened with starvation. The masses, it is delicately implied, must be kept in their place or they will reduce society to chaos. If you give them an inch they will take an ell. "Your people, sir, is a blind beast," said Alexander Hamilton. Though a founding father, he belonged to this stern school. He has a great many followers today and not all of them in the upper brackets. The WPA felt the full fury of their scorn. It was perhaps a natural reaction in Hamilton's time, when handicraft methods made wealth scarce, and there really was not enough to go around of anything except the barest essentials. It is not a natural reaction in an economy of abundance; it is a blind, unscientific, mean-spirited cultural lag. Hitler is said to share this view of the masses—and Hitler of all people should know better, considering the prodigies of work the German masses have performed for him.

Politically, any community which assumes that most of its members are unreliable anthropoids is on a shaky foundation, compared with a community which assumes that most of its members are inherently good people and only need a decent break to demonstrate their ability and their loyalty. Indeed the latter viewpoint reflects a democracy which cuts deeper than voting or democratic constitutions. You trust your fellow citizens or you do not trust them. The true democrat might be defined as one who assumes that other folks are as good as he is. If some do not appear to be as good he assumes that the trouble lies in their conditioning and not in any innate depravity. (By "good" he does not mean, of course, that all IQ's are equal.) Conditions can be changed, especially in an age of potential plenty. The idea of national minimums makes sense to true democrats. It deeply disturbs the opposite school.

Consumers First

The world revolution through which we are passing can be characterized as the tumultuous forward march of the "give 'em a break" idea. What Christian ethics, for all the devotion of its advocates, was never able to do, technology is now doing. Milo Perkins has phrased it thus:[1]

> We are engaged in a struggle that transcends the present war. This is a long, long fight to make a mass-production economy work. The battle started when machines became important in the lives of men. . . . It will be won when we have built up mass consumption to a point where markets can absorb the output of our mass production industries running at top speed. Then, so far as our physical needs are concerned, life can become a journey to be enjoyed rather than a battle to be fought.

It is hard to overemphasize the importance of the point which Milo Perkins raises. It is nothing less than a shift from production to consumption as the goal of high-energy societies. In building up our plant over the past two hundred years it has been inevitable that the producer should have first consideration. By "producer" I refer to those interests which have production in hand: business groups, organized farmers, promoters, investors in new industries, labor unions in recent years—in brief, the big pressure groups. Now the plant is built. After the war it will be superbuilt, as we have seen. Since the last war its potential output has been insufficiently utilized. During the depression the ratio of output to capacity was scandalously low, something in the order of 50 per cent. When the war is over large sections of the plant will just have to stand and rot unless we develop methods to get its fabulous output into the hands of the people—all the

1. Commencement address at Swarthmore College, May 25, 1942.

people.[2] Or unless we devote our efforts to perpetual warfare as an outlet for our abundance. A good case could be made for abundance as one cause of this revolutionary war—physical wealth that nations could not use except by blowing it up. Under this theory it is ironical that the war is developing still greater potential abundance. If we do not learn to use it, and quickly, it will sow the seeds of still greater wars.

The people, the consumers, the public interest must now come first. The prime motive of industry must no longer be to save, invest, accumulate wealth to enlarge the plant. The plant is large enough for all practical purposes. The prime motive of industry should now be to supply the community with the goods it needs. Men first, money second. Consumers first, producers second. That is what the revolution seems to be all about.

Years ago, in a book called *Economic Behavior,* C. E. Ayres made a comment on this subject which has haunted me ever since I read it:

> Presumably we build up capital, equipment, the means of the more extensive life by foregoing the full expenditure of our present resources at any given moment. But since we also propose to continue indefinitely to accumulate, the question ultimately arises: For what are we accumulating? At what moment in our economic history do we propose to cash in and enjoy the triumph of our thrift? But the answer is, never. There is no such moment. The motive of accumulation is not society's enjoyment. It is just perpetual accumulation.

2. The fact that the plant has been built to supply an adequate flow of goods to everybody does not mean that it should not be steadily improved. The point is, to change the accent from improvement as the first order of business—i.e., capital accumulation—to consumption as the first order of business. So long as inventors invent the plant is going to be improved.

Pursuing this goal we set up a series of financial institutions, including compound interest, which was the closest thing possible to a perpetual-accumulating machine. To have any final validity the flow of abstract numbers had to be paralleled with the brick and steel of physical plant. The plant did its best, but the laws of physics do not permit indefinite accumulation of brick and steel at compound-interest rates of growth. The formula had to run out sometime, and perhaps 1929 marked the year. When the turning point comes, a conscious shift from accumulation to consumption is the only way to keep the economy in balance. One might go farther and call it the only road to survival under power-age imperatives.

It is a curious track that Western communities have been on during the period of capital accumulation. It will deeply puzzle future historians. Everyone in his senses knows that the major purpose of an economic system should be to produce things the community needs.[3] But only in wartime has this purpose been deliberately served. At all other times from, say, 1750 to 1940, the major purpose of the system has been to provide money income for producers, and especially to reward those who saved and invested their money in new plant. It was assumed by orthodox students that this was the only right and moral way to produce the things the community needed. By concentrating on something other than the main purpose, the main purpose would be served.

It was served well when periods of prosperity rolled around. In periods of depression it was seriously neglected.

3. Said Adam Smith: "Consumption is the sole end and purpose of production; and the interest of the producer ought to be attended to only so far as may be necessary for promoting that of the consumer. The maxim is so perfectly self-evident that it would be absurd to attempt to prove it."

Finally, in the great depression, the dubious principle of hitting something by not aiming at it was so discredited, that governments everywhere were forced to move in to keep their citizens from mass hunger and despair.

Hereafter, unless I have completely misjudged the trend of the times and the temper of the people, economic systems are going to be run deliberately and directly for those ends which everybody knows they should be run for. We will use the front door, not the back.

The Statesman's Task

On the "give 'em a break" theory, the primary task of statesmanship is to keep all members loyal to the community and supplied with the essentials of life. The welfare of the community is paramount. What special-pressure groups would like to have is secondary. The statesmen must think of all essential industry as affected with a public interest.

From the physical viewpoint, the first charge on the total output of goods and services should be basic necessities for all citizens.

The second charge should be such mass comforts as are capable of quantity production. Prewar industry, for instance, could readily supply every family with a car, a radio, and plenty of trips to the movies. In this country it very nearly succeeded. Many mass comforts, as we noted earlier, are now in the class of necessities. They are the items which vary with population rather than with income.

The third charge might well be the construction and maintenance of those enduring works which all the people need and which may symbolize a great culture. The citizen of Athens saw the Acropolis and his spirit was lifted up. He was proud to be a member of a community which could produce such a just and lovely thing. No civilization can be reared without temples, pyramids, cathedrals, great public architecture, to dramatize its greatness to its people. In the Tennessee Valley we are evolving an architecture to fit our mighty engineering works that is as unprecedented as it is noble. It is also more useful than pyramids or temples.

The fourth and last charge on total output may be luxuries for the more fortunate groups—goods and services beyond the line of quantity production—jewels, country estates, custom-built motorcars, and the like. No civilization, not even Soviet Russia, has failed to provide a modicum of such luxuries for those at the top, whether they be kings, priests, tycoons or commissars. It would be unrealistic not to allow for them in postwar America. It might, however, be realistic to allow for not more than eight master bedrooms and a three-car garage.

Such are the classes of goods that all people want, that some people want, and that a great civilization demands. They are the classes of goods the statesmen should plan to have produced, and in that order. They represent the normal procedure for a genuine economy of abundance. We may or may not attain such a structural arrangement after the war, but sooner or later, some power-age community, if not America, will attain it. It is on the cards; it is what the people of the Western world are after. They know that modern technology can provide the output. They know that their economic misery in recent years has been a needless waste. They will not rest, or give their leaders rest, until the possible is made the actual.

Starting on the Ground Floor

Observe that competition for place in the social order is not banished from an economy devoted to these ends. It is simply moved above the ground floor. The penalty of bad luck, of an inadequate education, of an Act of God, of an IQ below 100, is no longer a bread line, a flophouse or a leap from Brooklyn Bridge. A base is cemented home below which no American need ever go. Competition begins at that base. Citizens can still battle for positions in the upper stories, namely, preferred calls on the output of luxuries. But when the losers come tumbling downstairs they no longer fall into the cellar. They pick themselves up, wipe off the blood, and start again on the ground floor. Their wives and children do not have to pay the unjust and dreadful penalties that wives and children have paid throughout the great depression.

Observe further that in drawing this physical picture there has been little talk of free enterprise or government enterprise. There has only been talk of community needs and community output. In this frame of reference no one gives a tinker's damn whether needed shelter is built by the U.S. Housing Authority or by John Strong, Inc.—so long as it is soundly built. We are getting plenty of exercise in this point of view right now. No one gives a tinker's damn whether the New London Navy Yard or the Electric Boat Company builds submarines, so long as they are well and quickly built.

We are being exercised in the whole philosophy of physical economics. Of our total national output, some 50 per cent or more will soon be allocated to war purposes. The balance is allocated to consumers, with equal sharing, through rationing, for many items. Luxury output is forced out of production to a large extent, and long-term public works are postponed. The order of planned output in 1942 is:

1. Munitions of war.
2. Basic essentials for all citizens.
3. A few mass comforts—movies, tobacco, certain items of clothing.

A Mixed Economy

One of the best things the war could do for us would be to break down permanently the habit of judging public or private enterprise as either all white or all black, depending on one's point of view. We are, I think, heading deeper into a mixed economy, where government takes the responsibility of over-all planning for full employment, but where big business, little business, co-operative associations, and that vast zone of nonprofit enterprise—churches, clubs, foundations, universities and the like—all share the field. In such an economy, citizens should keep their attention fixed on *ends to be served,* and use whatever means seem best to achieve them. Big industry is good at mass production, provided its executives devote their talents to production and not restriction. Perhaps we can rely on Thurman Arnold to keep them pointed in the right direction. Little industry is good along Main Street. Co-operatives are good for many of the needs of farmers and consumers. Foundations and universities are good for promoting science and research.[4]

Economic theologists of the right and left, who say we must have complete free enterprise or go completely total-

4. In a future book in this series we will examine the mixed-economy idea at some length.

itarian, or who say we must have complete socialism or be overwhelmed by the plutocrats, will have nowhere to lay their heads in a mixed economy. It is *not* the authoritarian state and it is *not* the automatic free enterprise system. It is rather the application of plain common sense, using all available agencies to do what needs to be done. The hope of getting a hearing for a little common sense has hitherto been remote, but the war is beginning to clear the air of a lot of ideological nonsense.

We come back finally to the image of the national family, with Pa, Ma and the children on the ranch. The rights and duties of citizens, full employment, the budget of essentials, are not difficult to manage administratively or mentally when one thinks of all Americans as one great family. They are very difficult if not impossible to manage when one thinks of Americans as isolated individuals, each on the make, and not much to be trusted.

Traditionally most of us have held the latter outlook, especially those of us born before 1900. The expanding frontier, the folklore of the pioneer, have conditioned our minds in that direction. "Ungoverned and ungovernable" we have been called as a nation, and with some justice. We have often thought of our fellow citizens as competitors, as strong men to be humbled, as low fellows to be kept in their place. We have not thought of them as part of us.

Now the geographic frontiers have gone, and a new kind of pioneering lies before us. The power age with its specialization has made us dependent one upon the other as the old pioneer never was. Depression and war have forced us to realize that we must sink or swim together as one community. We have turned a solid face toward our enemies abroad. By this very act we have turned a friendly face toward our neighbors at home . . . our people, Americans.